McGraw-Hill
My World of KNOWLEDGE

Includes: Atlas, Dictionary, and Encyclopedia

Written by
Kay Barnham and Robin Lawrie

Illustrated by
Robin Lawrie

PART 1

YOUNG LEARNER'S ATLAS

CONTENTS

All About Maps	2	C.I.S.	22
World Map	4	Africa	24
Around The World	6	The Middle East	26
The Changing World	8	Southern Asia	28
People of the World	10	Southeast Asia	30
U.S.A.	12	East Asia	32
Canada	14	Australia and New Zealand	34
Central America	15	Arctic	36
North America	16	Antarctica	37
South America	18	World Facts	38
Europe	20	Index	40

McGraw-Hill Consumer Products

All About Maps

A map is a picture of a place seen from far above.

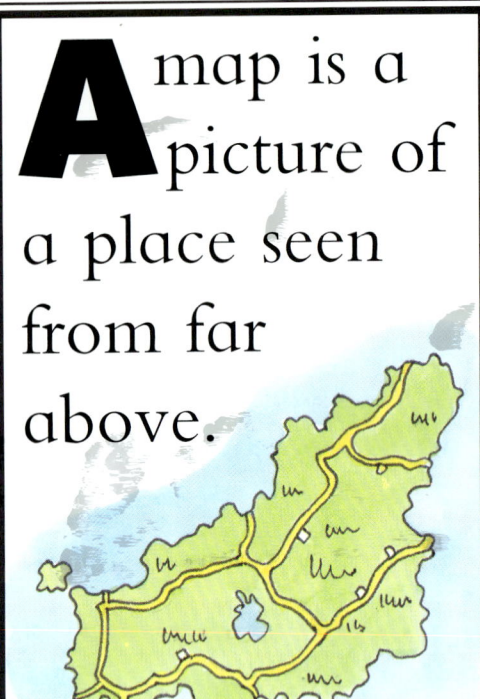

A book of maps is called an atlas. It shows maps of every country in the world.

Watch for the mini-map of the world to see where each country belongs.

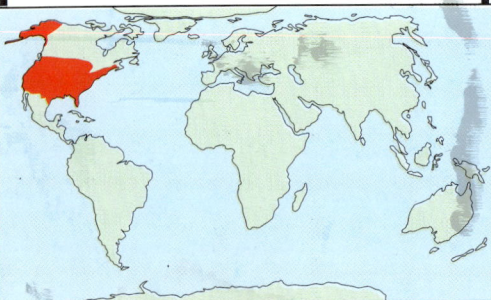

Maps can show places from near or far away.

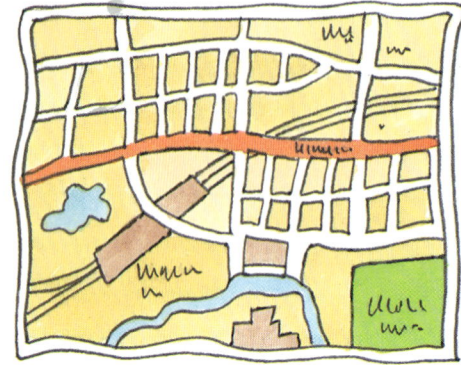

Some maps are so detailed that they show all the streets in a town or city.

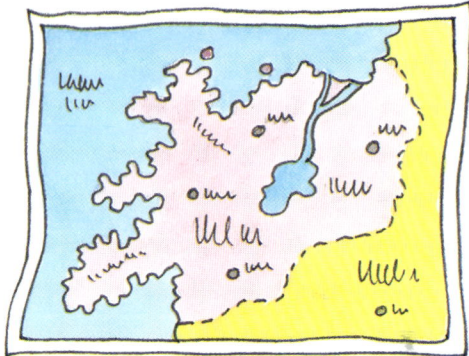

Maps of whole countries are shown from far away. Dots show where towns and cities are.

Maps cannot copy the real size of the places they show. They are drawn to a scale, which means that they are shrunk to fit the page.

MILES	250	500	1000
KILOMETERS	250	500	1000

A small distance on a map stands for a much larger distance in real life. The distance is shown under each map on a scale bar, which shows miles and kilometers.

The symbols below are used on the maps in this book.

Borders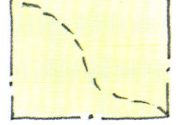

Capital cities

Large cities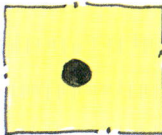

Lakes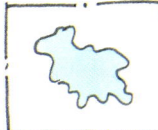

Rivers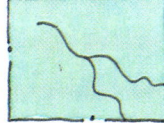

Oceans and seas

Mountains

Find out where different animals live in the world. Look for them on each map.

Explorers and travelers use maps to find their way.

You can use maps to see where you live in the world, or perhaps where you are going on vacation.

The index on page 40 has an alphabetical list of all the countries in the world. It tells you where to find each country in this atlas.

There is a compass beside every map in this book. This is to show you in which direction the map is facing.

North points to the top of the world and South points to the bottom of the world.

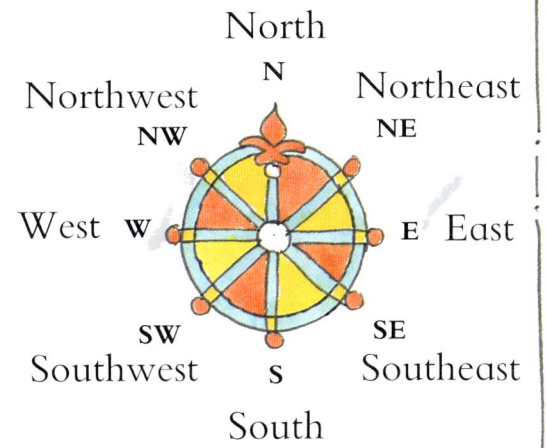

3

WORLD MAP

This is what the world would look like if it were flattened out. The seven colored areas are called continents.

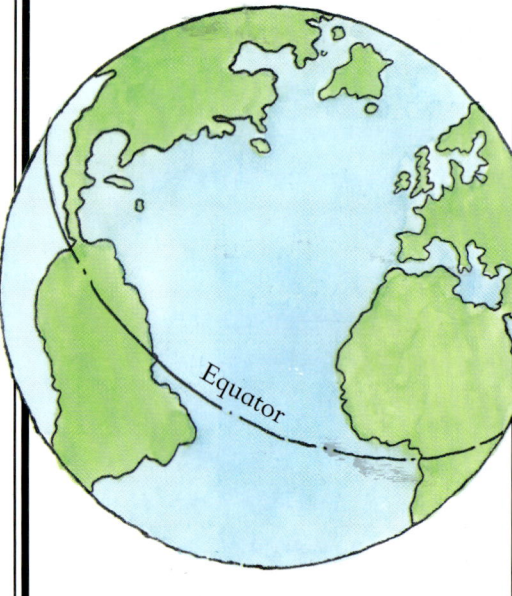

The Equator is an imaginary line running round the middle of the world, which divides it into northern and southern hemispheres. The U.S.A. is in the northern hemisphere.

North America stretches from the Arctic almost to the Equator.

Polar bear

Moose

Beaver

NORTH AMERICA

Atlantic Ocean

Native American totem pole

Bald eagle

U.S. Capitol Building

Atlantic flying fish

Mayan pyramid, Mexico

Equator

Toucan

Pacific Ocean

South American macaw

SOUTH AMERICA

Giant statues, Easter Island

Blue whale

N
NW NE
W E
SW SE
S

Most of South America is below the Equator.

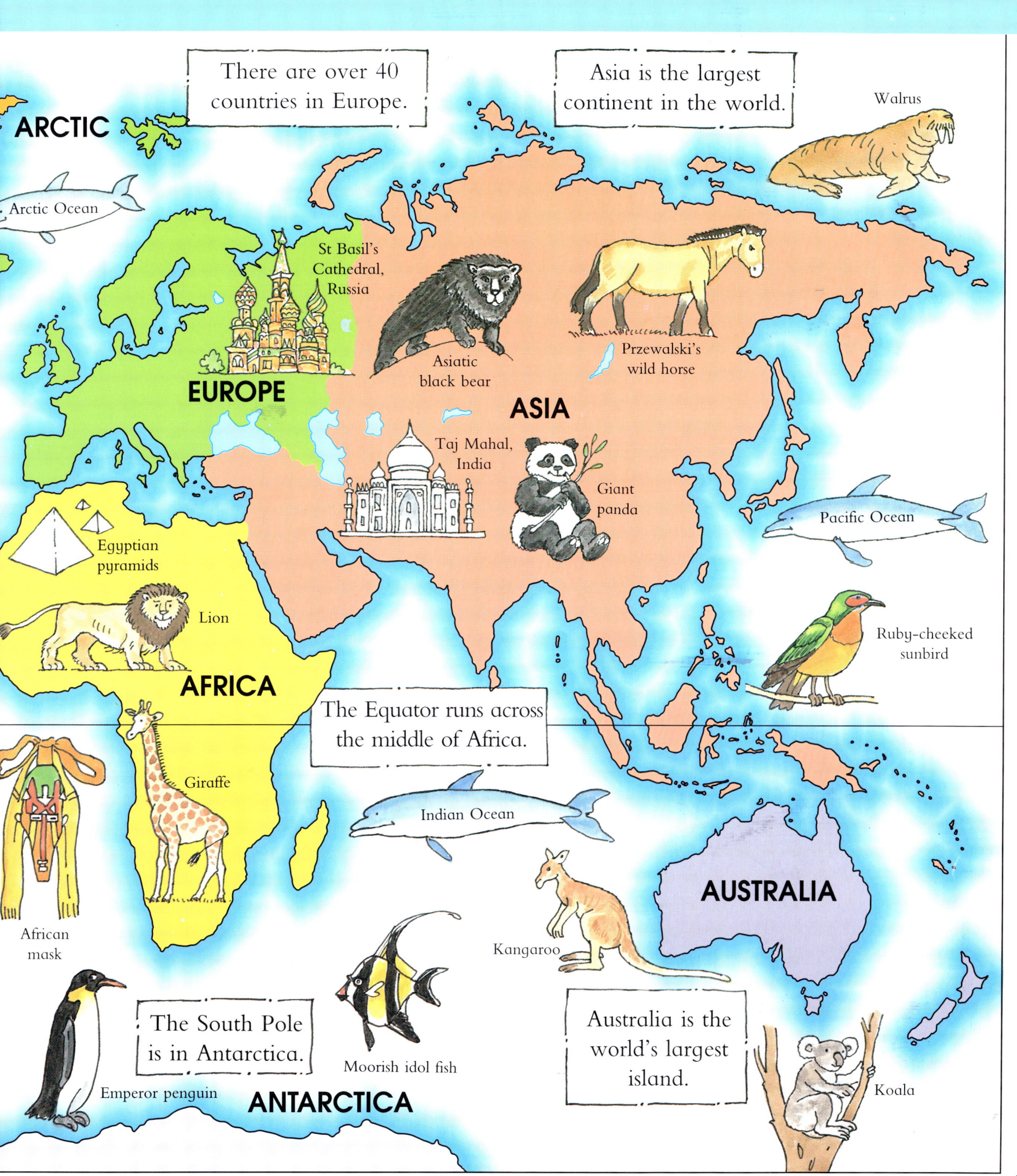

Around The World

The surface of the Earth is different all over the world. Over two-thirds is covered with water. Inside the Earth, there are layers. As these move, heat can build up and cause volcanic eruptions.

Glaciers are frozen rivers of ice, which slide slowly downhill. Some glaciers move only a tiny fraction a day.

Canyons are formed when rivers slowly wash the rock away. The Grand Canyon in the U.S.A. is more than a mile deep!

Geysers are hot springs that shoot hot water into the air. The most famous geyser is found in Yellowstone Park, U.S.A. It is called "Old Faithful."

Coral reefs are formed in warm, shallow seas from the skeletons of millions of tiny sea creatures. The Great Barrier Reef, in Australia, is the largest.

The Changing World

The Earth was formed more than 4.5 billion years ago. Its surface was molten rock.

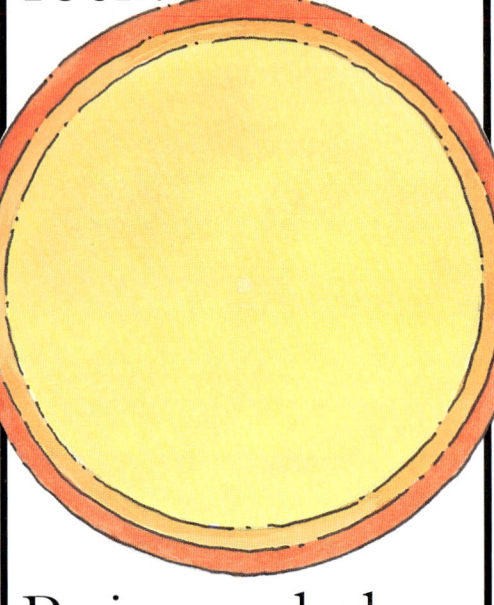

Rain cooled and hardened the Earth. The water formed shallow seas.

About 200 million years ago the continents were all joined together and surrounded by one vast ocean.

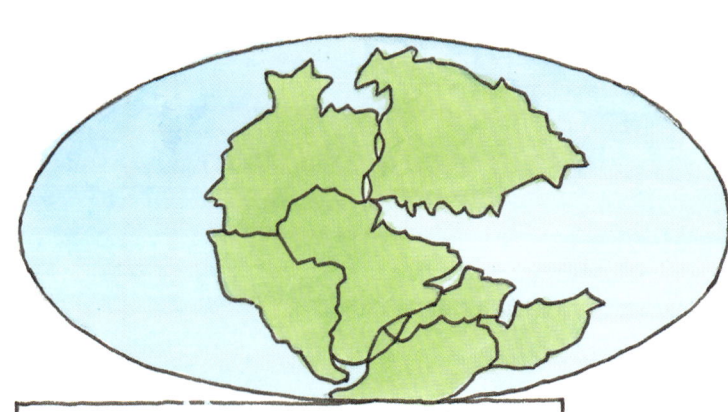

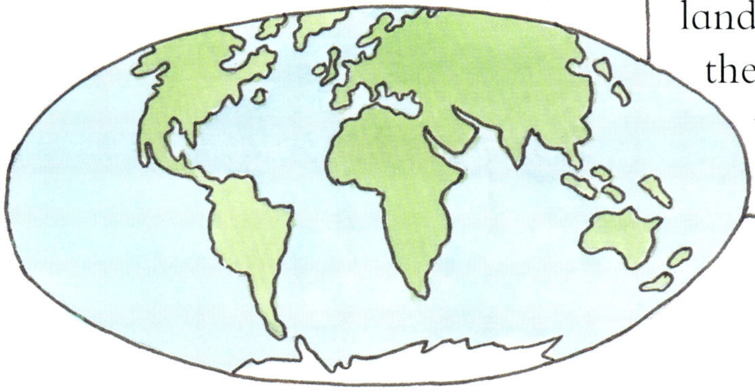

Slowly, the land areas drifted apart, and over millions of years, continents formed. The land is still moving. In the future, inland seas will widen to become an ocean.

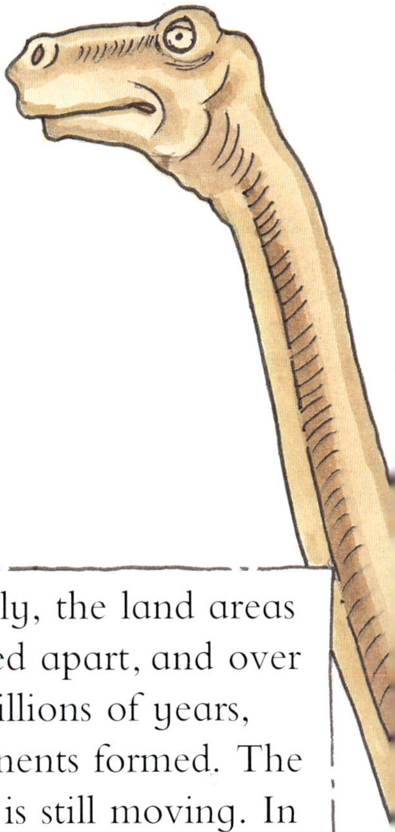

Large chunks of land, called plates, move by floating on a layer of hot, molten rock.

Fossils are traces of early life found in rocks. They help us find out about living things from long ago.

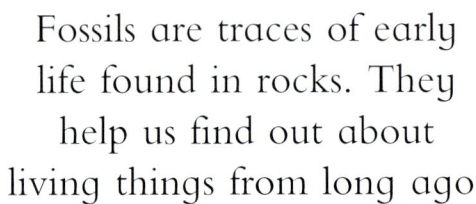
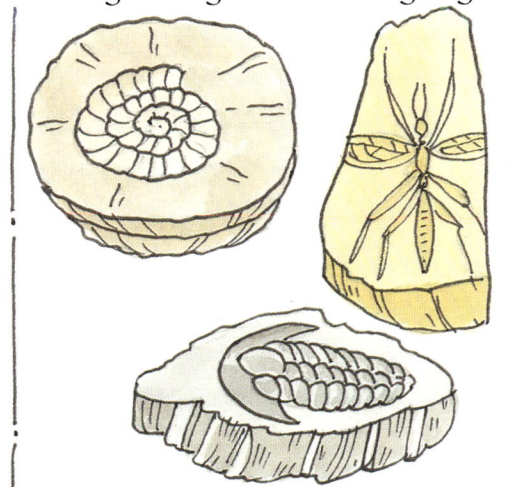

PEOPLE OF THE WORLD

Here you can see traditional costumes that are still worn on special festival days around the world. Learn how people say "hello" in different languages, too.

There are over 5,000 languages. If you learn to speak different languages, you can speak to people all around the world.

France
"Bonjour" (French)

Italy
"Ciao" (Italian)

Denmark
"Halloj" (Danish)

Poland
"Dzien dobry" (Polish)

Greece
"Yia sas" (Greek)

India
"Namaste" (Hindi)

Some alphabets use different letters, and Chinese and Japanese alphabets have "picture writing" instead. There are over 65 different alphabets.

ΣΩΘ ЖФΨ 人四下

UNITED STATES OF AMERICA

The United States of America is so wide that it crosses eight time zones.

When it is afternoon in New York, it is morning in Hawaii.

The huge Boeing factory at Seattle makes many of the world's airliners.

Zuni corn dancer, Hopi tribe, New Mexico

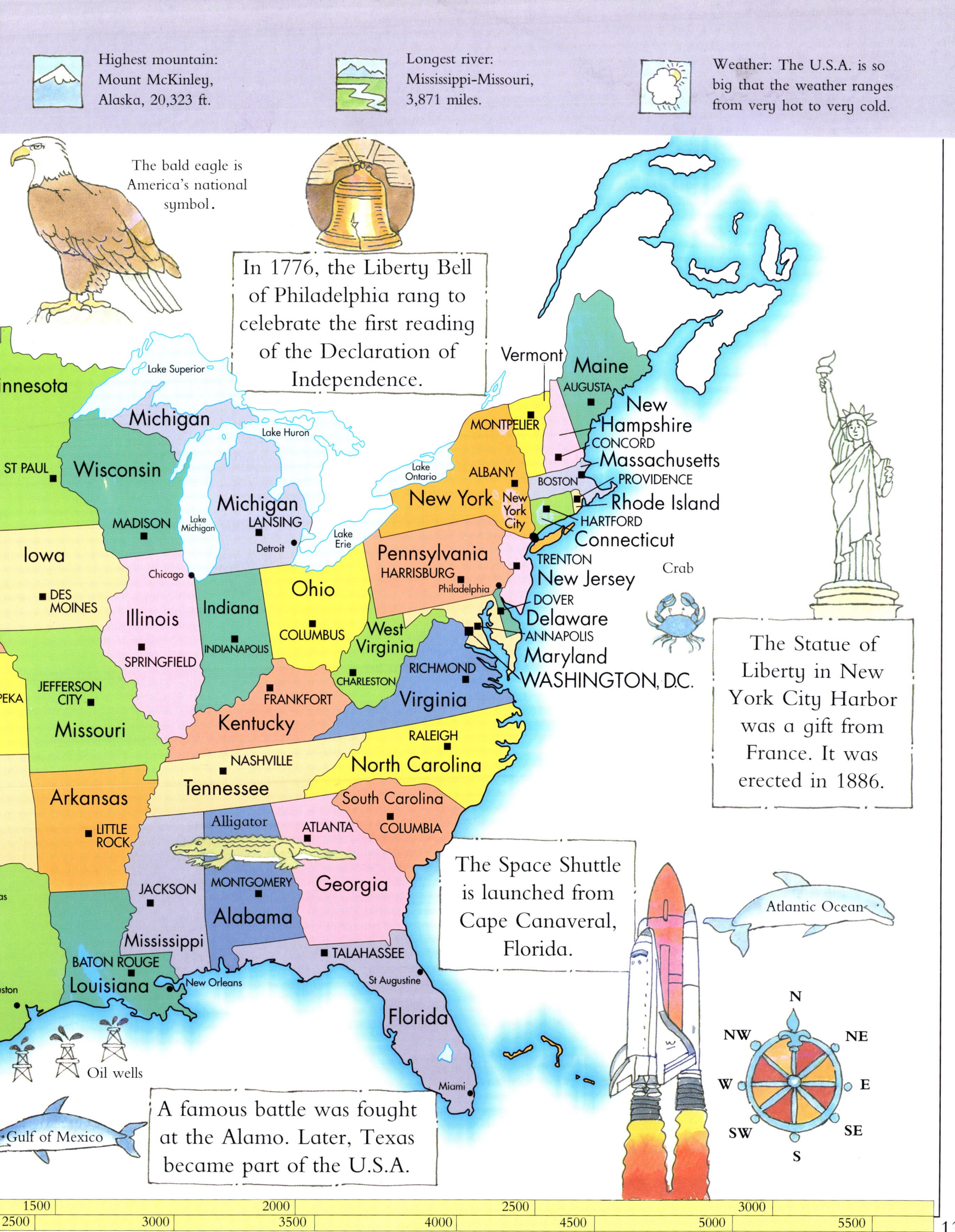

CANADA

 Highest mountain: Mount Logan, 19,525 ft.

 Longest river: Mackenzie, 2,635 miles.

Canada is the second-largest country in the world, but has only one-ninth of the population of the United States.

Canada has ten provinces and two federal territories.

Mountain goat

GREENLAND

Arctic fox

Ice fishing

Mount Logan
YUKON
WHITEHORSE
Mackenzie River
Great Bear Lake
NORTHWEST TERRITORIES
Yellowknife
Great Slave Lake
Baffin Island
CANADA
Atlantic Ocean
Prince Rupert
Peace River
Lake Athabasca
Hudson Bay
Goose Bay
NEWFOUNDLAND AND LABRADOR
BRITISH COLUMBIA
ALBERTA
Rocky Mountains
EDMONTON
SASKATCHEWAN
MANITOBA
Lake Winnipeg
NEWFOUNDLAND (ISLAND)
ST. JOHN'S
Vancouver
Calgary
Saskatoon
ONTARIO
Charlottetown
PRINCE EDWARD ISLAND
VICTORIA
REGINA
WINNIPEG
Lake Superior
The Great Lakes
QUEBEC
Fredericton
NOVA SCOTIA
Halifax
NEW BRUNSWICK
Lake Michigan
Montreal
OTTAWA
TORONTO
Lake Ontario
Lake Huron
Lake Erie

Native American totem pole

The St. Lawrence Seaway links the Atlantic Ocean with the Great Lakes.

The Royal Canadian Mounted Police is Canada's national police force.

Canadian maple syrup is made from sap that drips from maple trees.

Killer whales are found along the Pacific Coast.

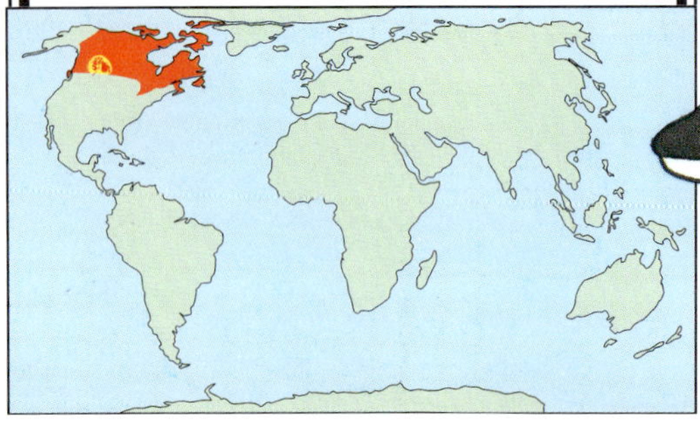

Ice hockey is very popular in Canada.

MILES	250	500	1000	1500	2000	2500	3000
KILOMETERS		1000	1500	2000	2500	3000	3500	4000	4500	5000

Central America

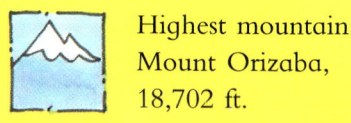
Highest mountain: Mount Orizaba, 18,702 ft.

Mexico and Central America link the U.S.A. and South America.

Mexico is the largest country in this region. Much of the country is very high, dry, and rocky.

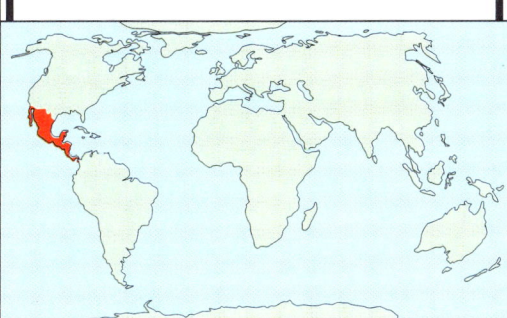

Spicy Mexican food, such as tacos and chili con carne, is popular all over the world.

More than 20 million people are crowded into Mexico City.

Jai alai is the world's fastest ball game.

Most of Mexico's oil comes from under the sea.

Aztec, Mayan, and Toltec people once ruled Mexico. Some of their temples remain.

The Panama Canal connects the Atlantic and Pacific Oceans. It can shorten a sea journey by thousands of miles.

MILES	250	500	1000	1500	2000
KILOMETERS	500	1000	1500	2000	2500	3000	3500

North America

North America stretches from the Canadian Arctic down to Panama.

It includes the U.S.A., Canada, Mexico, and the countries of Central America.

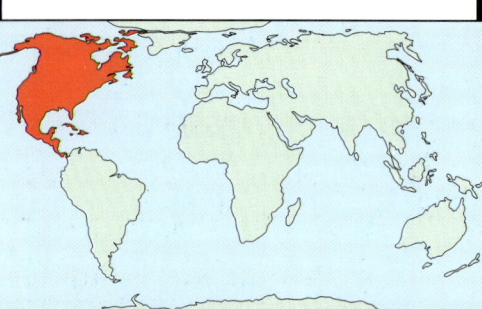

Plains (Sioux)

Southwest (Hopi)

Northwest coast (Chilkat)

Native Americans lived in North America for thousands of years before European settlers arrived.

One Californian giant sequoia tree is 276 feet tall and over 2,200 years old.

Oui! Yes!

Canada has two official languages—French and English.

The Pacific coast of North America is usually mild and wet in winter.

In Canada, snowshoes are used to walk on deep snow.

Wild horses, called broncos, are ridden by cowboys at rodeos. One famous rodeo is the Calgary Stampede in Alberta, Canada.

MILES	250	500	1000	1500	2000	2500	3000
KILOMETERS	500	1000	1500	2000	2500	3000	3500	4000	4500	500

SOUTH AMERICA

In the early 1500s, Spanish and Portuguese settlers arrived in South America. They conquered the native people.

Now a mix of Indians, Africans and Europeans live there.

Giant tortoises live on the Galápagos Islands.

Galápagos Islands

Rivers and streams feed into the mighty Amazon River from an area ten times as big as France. This area is called the Amazon Basin and covers parts of Brazil, Peru, and Colombia.

This area has more species of living things than anywhere else in the world. There are over 50,000 types of plants!

Andean cock-of-the-rock

Pacific Ocean

Farmers, lumberjacks, and miners clear huge areas of rainforest every day. Without trees, the soil is soon washed away by heavy rain, leaving barren ground where nothing grows.

The Capybara, a relative of the guinea pig, is the world's largest rodent. It is over three feet long!

MILES	250	500	1000	1500	2000	2500
KILOMETERS	500	1000	1500	2000	2500	3000	3500	4000

EUROPE

Europe is about the same size as the U.S.A., but has nearly three times as many people. There are many different cultures, and more than 40 languages are spoken.

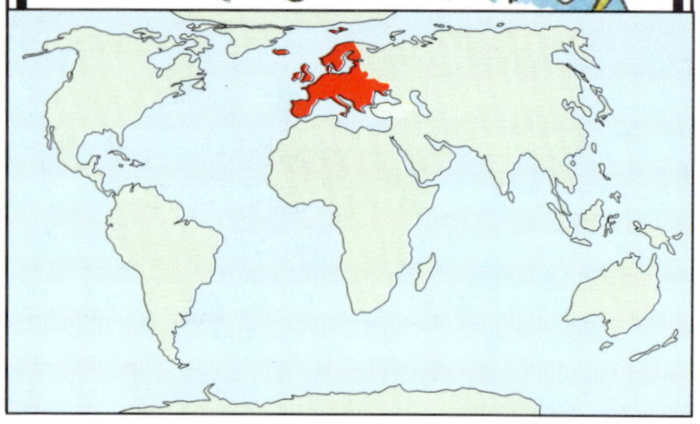

The Netherlands is known for growing beautiful tulips.

Atlantic Ocean

Historic Britain has many famous landmarks.

Swiss clock makers are famous for their skills.

Many famous painters lived in France. The country is well known for its wine and cheese.

Highland dancing

Flamenco dancers

Leaning Tower of Pisa, Italy

MILES	250	500		1000	
KILOMETERS		500	1000	1500	2000

C.I.S.

C.I.S. stands for the Commonwealth of Independent States. It was formed from parts of the Union of Soviet Socialist Republics in 1991.

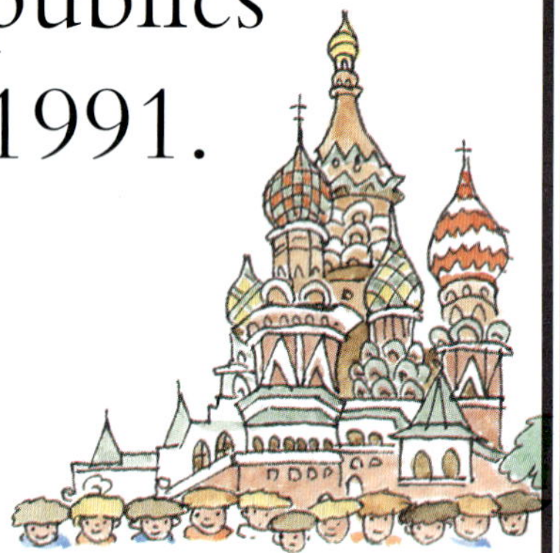

Russia is the biggest country in the world.

Moscow is the home of the famous Bolshoi Ballet dancers. They have performed all over the world.

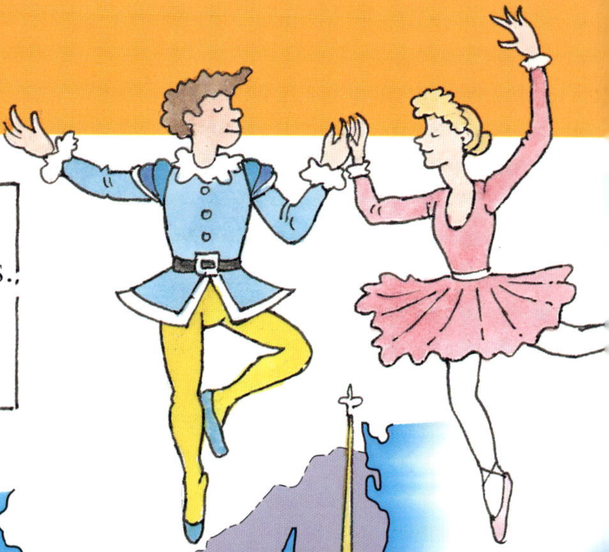

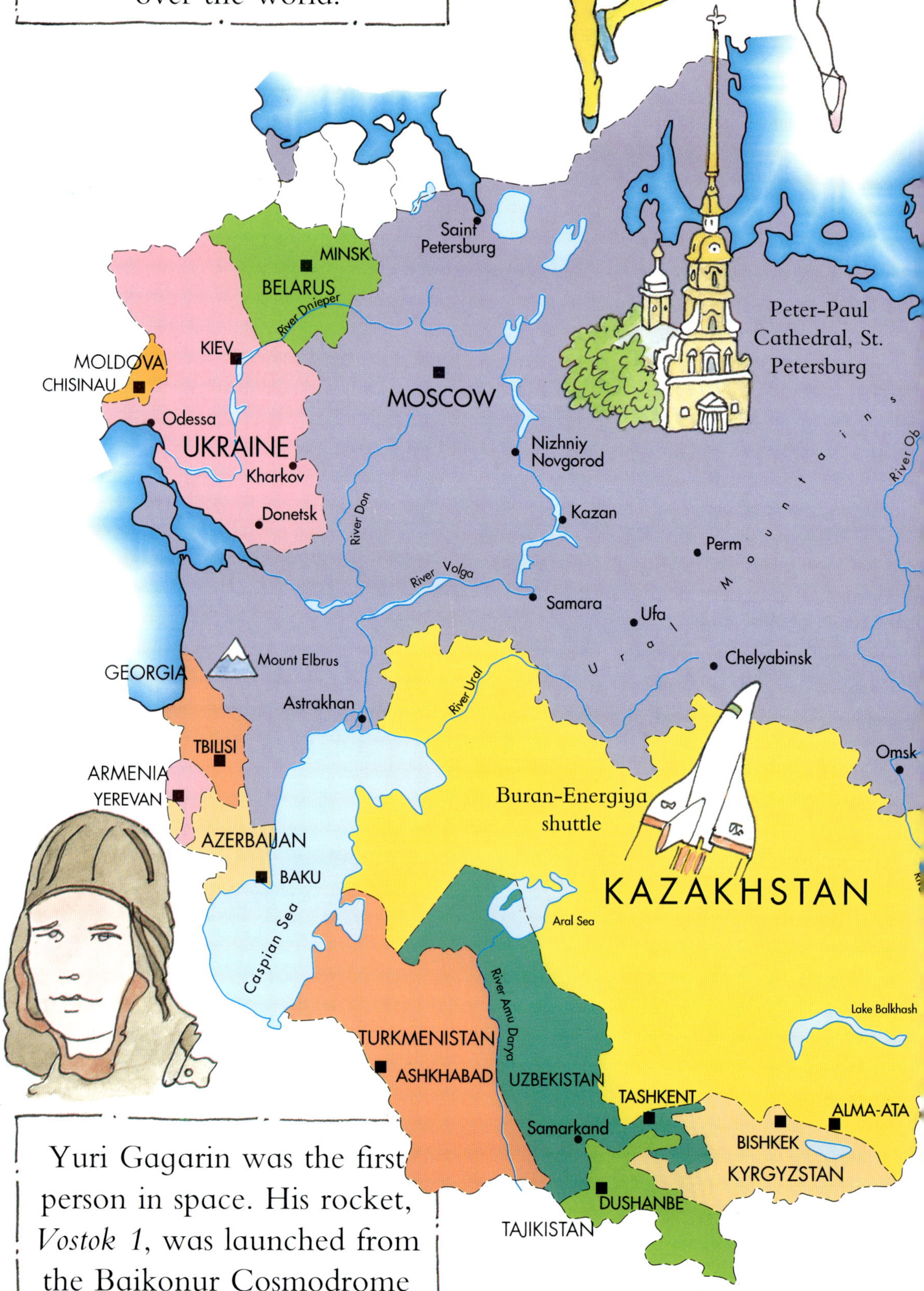

Yuri Gagarin was the first person in space. His rocket, *Vostok 1*, was launched from the Baikonur Cosmodrome in Kazakhstan.

Miles	250	500	1000		
Kilometers	500	1000	1500	2000	

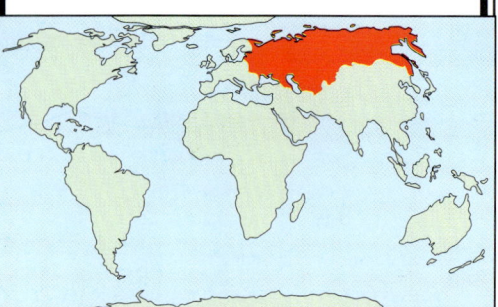

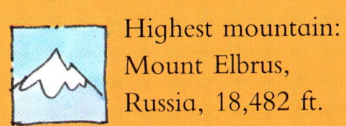 Highest mountain: Mount Elbrus, Russia, 18,482 ft.

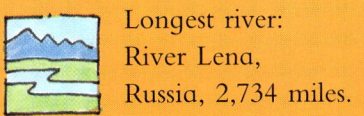 Longest river: River Lena, Russia, 2,734 miles.

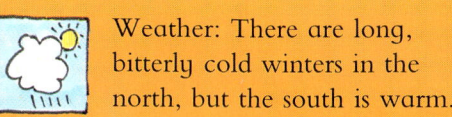 Weather: There are long, bitterly cold winters in the north, but the south is warm.

The north is very cold in the winter months. Temperatures in Siberia can sometimes reach −26°F.

The Siberian coast is only 55 miles from mainland Alaska.

There are over 250 volcanoes on the Kamchatka Peninsula and nearby islands.

The Trans-Siberian Railway runs from Moscow to Vladivostok. It is the longest railway in the world!

Lake Baykal is the deepest lake in the world. One part is 6,365 feet deep!

Africa

There are about 670 million people in Africa—over twice the number of people in the United States.

The world's largest desert is the Sahara Desert in Africa.

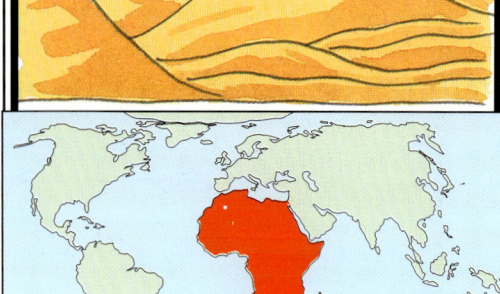

Madeira Island (Portugal)

Canary Islands (Spain)

About 800 languages are spoken in Africa.

Ivory Coast grows more cacao beans than any other country.

Cacao fruit

Cacao flower

Atlantic Ocean

Fruit, vegetables, and crafts are sold in village markets.

Many Africans are now leaving the villages to go and work in large cities.

Diamonds are mined in South Africa.

RABAT • ALGIERS • TUNISIA • TRIPOLI
MOROCCO • Atlas Mountains • ALGERIA • Hoopoe
AL AAIUN • WESTERN SAHARA • Camel • Haggar Mountains
Fennel fox • MAURITANIA • MALI • Jerboa
NOUAKCHOTT • NIGER
DAKAR • THE GAMBIA • SENEGAL • BAMAKO • NIAMEY
BANJUL • BISSAU • BURKINA FASO
GUINEA-BISSAU • GUINEA • OUAGADOUGOU • NIGERIA • ABUJA
CONAKRY • FREETOWN • SIERRA LEONE • IVORY COAST • GHANA • BENIN • TOGO • Lagos • River Benue
MONROVIA • LIBERIA • ABIDJAN • ACCRA • LOMÉ • PORTO-NOVO • CAMEROON
MALABO • EQUATORIAL GUINEA • YAOUNDÉ
LIBREVILLE • GABON
CABINDA (ANGOLA)
LUANDA

River Niger

MILES	250	500		1000	
KILOMETERS		500	1000	1500	2000

24

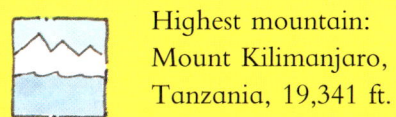 Highest mountain: Mount Kilimanjaro, Tanzania, 19,341 ft.

 Longest river: River Nile, Egypt, 4,132 miles.

 Weather: It is hot and humid at the Equator. The deserts in the north are very hot and dry.

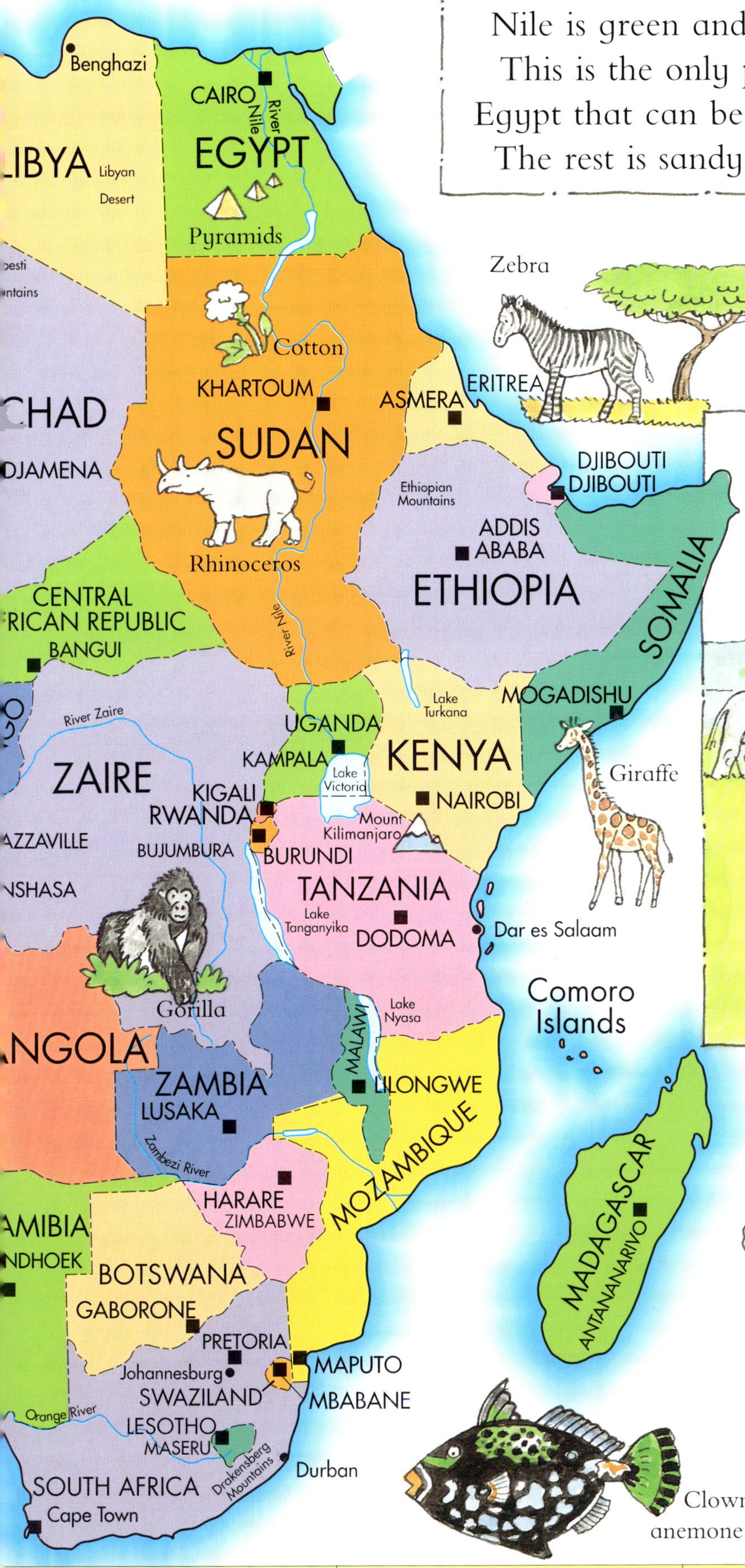

The land around the River Nile is green and fertile. This is the only part of Egypt that can be farmed. The rest is sandy desert.

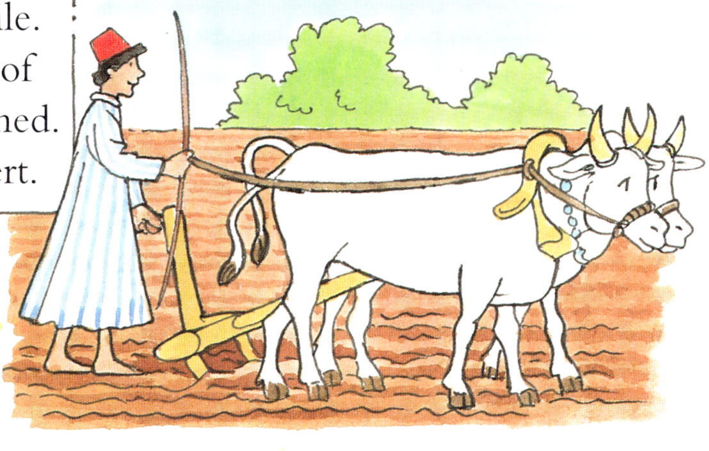

Africa still has herds of wild animals. They graze on the grasslands of the savannah.

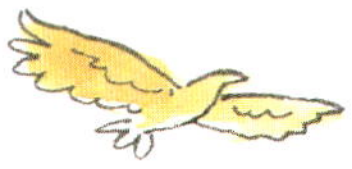

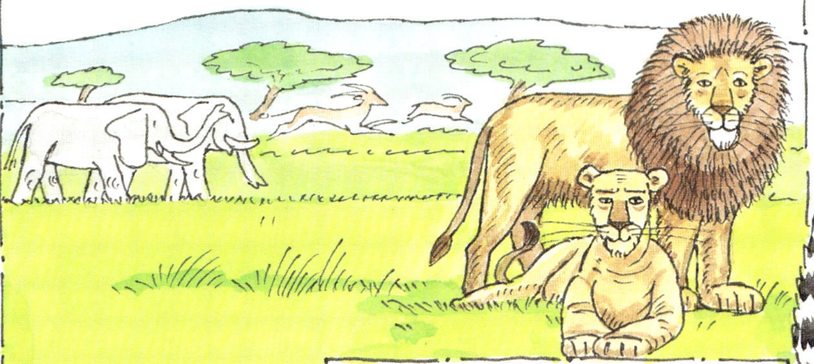

Many wild animals live in wildlife preserves to protect them.

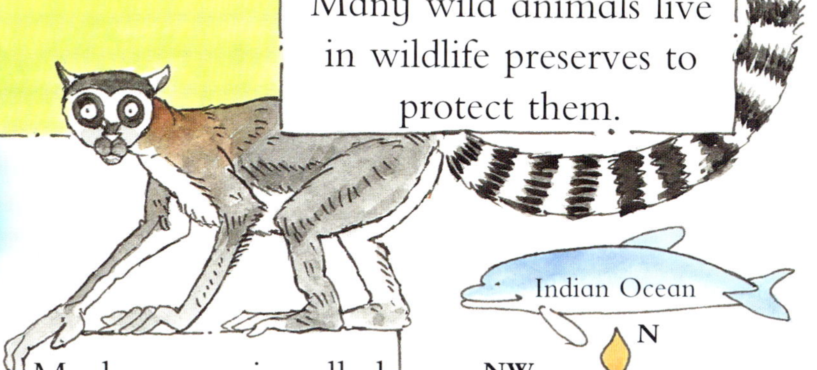

Madagascar is called the "Red Island" because of its red soil. It is the home of the lemur.

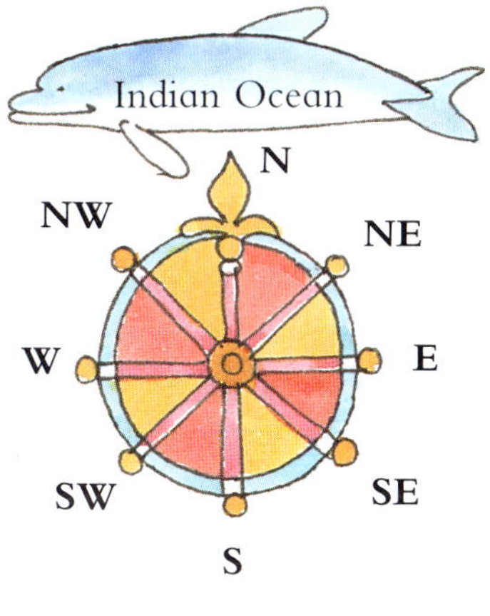

The Middle East

Most of the Middle East is covered with desert and mountains.

There is lots of valuable oil under the desert and seabed. Oil is sold to other countries to use as fuel.

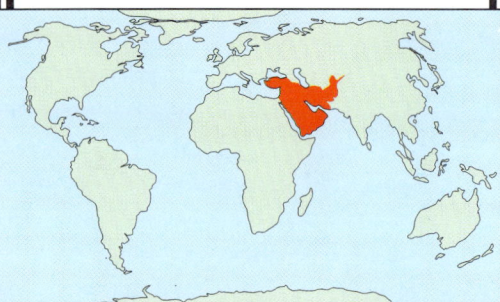

Jerusalem in Israel is a holy city for Christians, Jews, and Muslims.

Dome of the Rock

Only Muslims visit the sacred city of Mecca in Saudi Arabia.

The Kabah

Arab "dhow"

A falconer

Bedouin people

The Rub' al Khali desert in Saudi Arabia covers almost a quarter of the country. It is the largest stretch of sand in the world.

Black Sea

Istanbul · Ankara
TURKEY
Izmir
Marjoram
Olives
Taurus Mountains
Melons
River Euphrates
River Tigres

Nicosia
CYPRUS
Mediterranean Sea
LEBANON
BEIRUT
SYRIA
DAMASCUS
BAGHDAD
IRAQ
ISRAEL
Tel Aviv
JERUSALEM
AMMAN
JORDAN

SAUDI ARABIA
Jedda
Mecca
Hijaz

Arabian Sea

MILES	250	500	1000	
KILOMETERS	500	1000	1500	2000

| 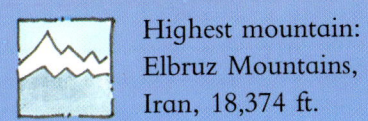 Highest mountain: Elbruz Mountains, Iran, 18,374 ft. | 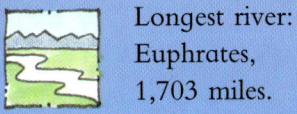 Longest river: Euphrates, 1,703 miles. |  Weather: These countries have hot, dry summers, but in the north, the winters are often cold. |

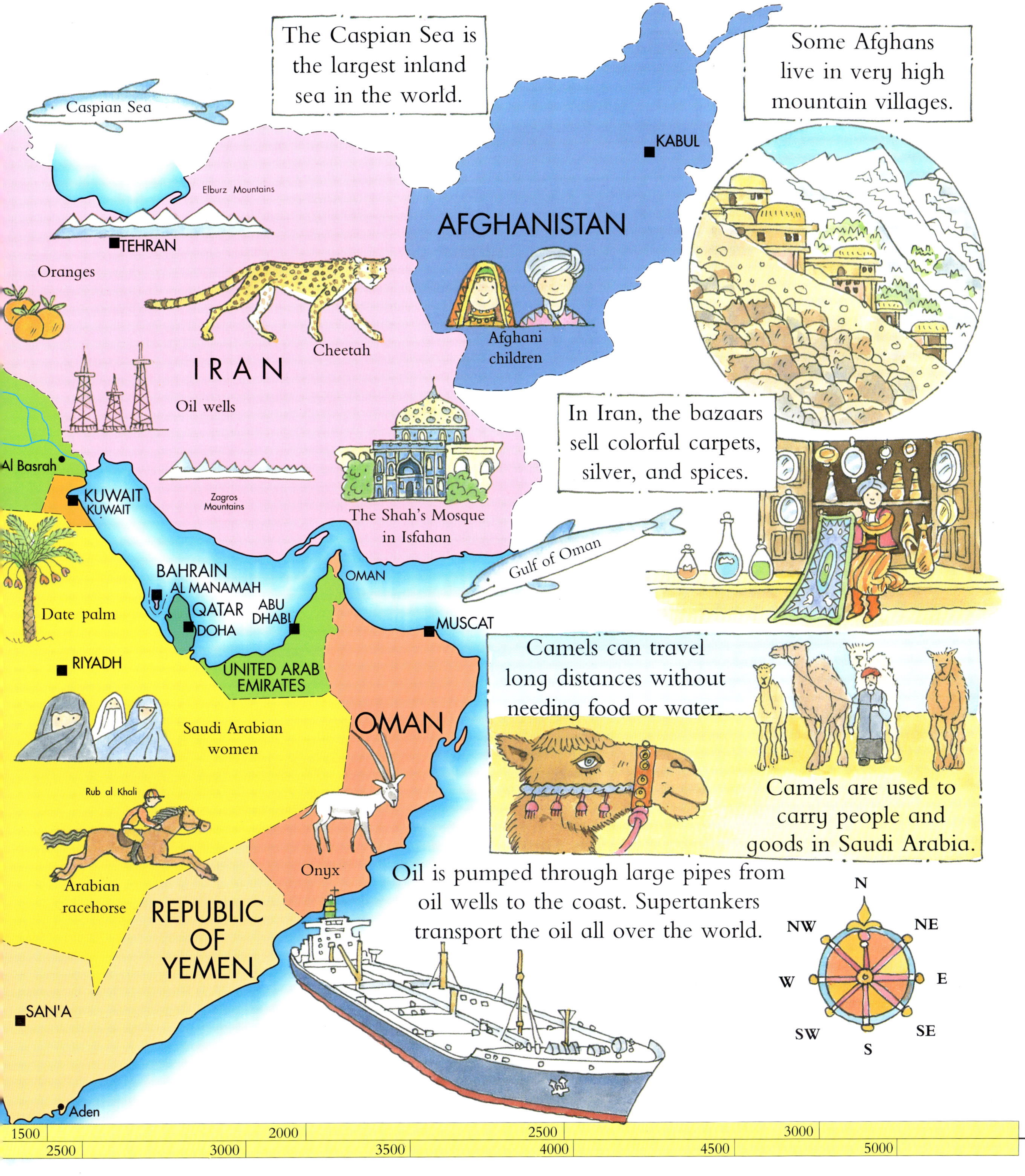

The Caspian Sea is the largest inland sea in the world.

Some Afghans live in very high mountain villages.

Caspian Sea

Elburz Mountains

TEHRAN

Oranges

Cheetah

KABUL

AFGHANISTAN

Afghani children

IRAN

Oil wells

In Iran, the bazaars sell colorful carpets, silver, and spices.

Al Basrah

KUWAIT
KUWAIT

Zagros Mountains

The Shah's Mosque in Isfahan

Gulf of Oman

BAHRAIN
AL MANAMAH
QATAR
DOHA
ABU DHABI

OMAN

MUSCAT

Date palm

UNITED ARAB EMIRATES

Camels can travel long distances without needing food or water.

RIYADH

Saudi Arabian women

OMAN

Rub al Khali

Camels are used to carry people and goods in Saudi Arabia.

Arabian racehorse

Onyx

REPUBLIC OF YEMEN

Oil is pumped through large pipes from oil wells to the coast. Supertankers transport the oil all over the world.

SAN'A

Aden

```
        N
   NW       NE
 W             E
   SW       SE
        S
```

| 1500 | 2000 | 2500 | 3000 |
| 2500 | 3000 | 3500 | 4000 | 4500 | 5000 |

27

Southern Asia

Asian farmers rely on the important monsoon rains to make their crops grow.

If there is too much rain, floods can destroy crops and villages.

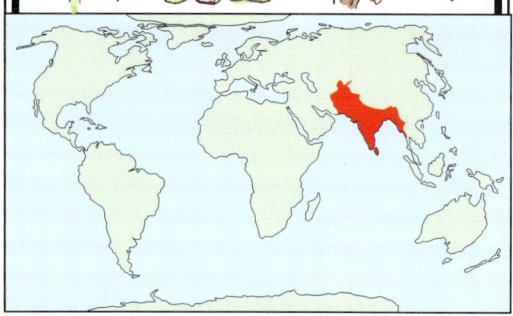

Rice Tea Coffee

One-fifth of Afghanistan's people are nomads. They wander from place to place.

KABUL
AFGHANISTAN
ISLAMABAD
Rawalpindi
Afghan "ghadi"
Lahore
Blackbuck
River Indus
Thar Desert
PAKISTAN
Indian elephant
Karachi
Ahmadabad
Bombay

Pakistan's official language is Urdu.

The Taj Mahal, near New Delhi in India, is made of marble. It is the tomb of an Indian emperor's wife.

More tea is grown in India than in any other country in the world.

Leaves from tea plants are picked, dried, and crushed into tea leaves.

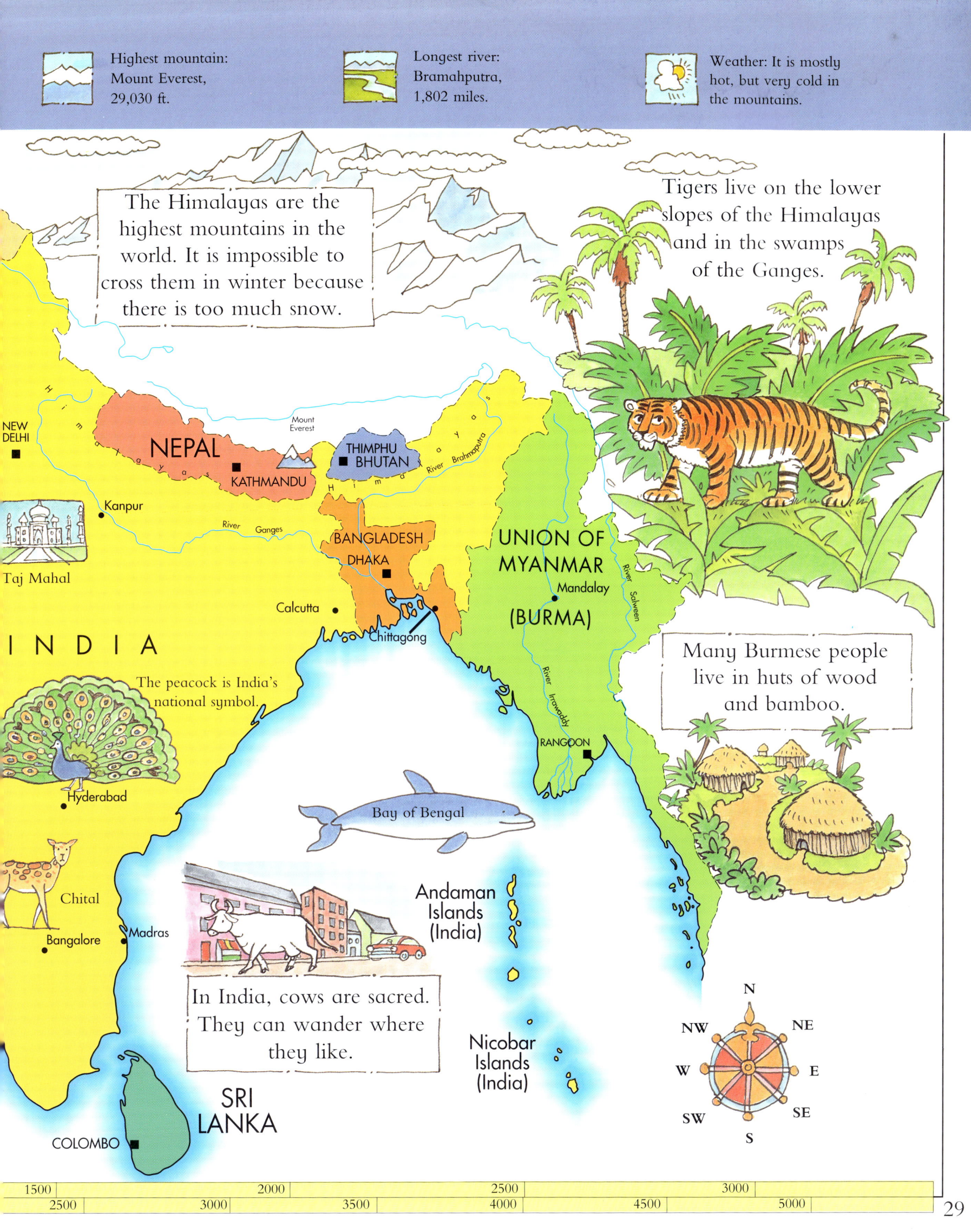

SOUTHEAST ASIA AND PACIFIC

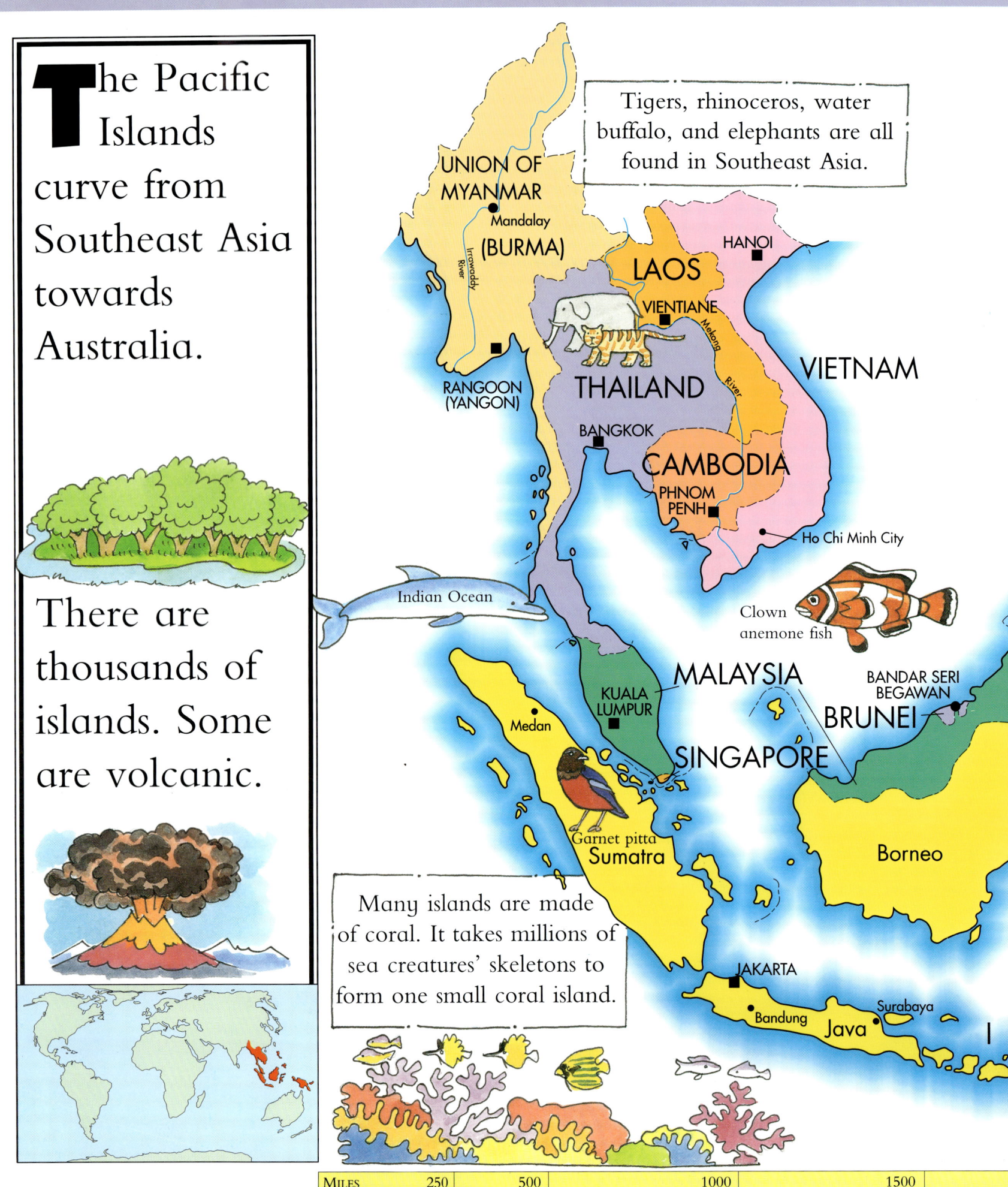

The Pacific Islands curve from Southeast Asia towards Australia.

There are thousands of islands. Some are volcanic.

Tigers, rhinoceros, water buffalo, and elephants are all found in Southeast Asia.

Many islands are made of coral. It takes millions of sea creatures' skeletons to form one small coral island.

ISLANDS

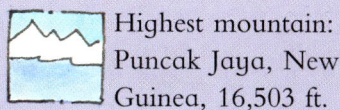 Highest mountain: Puncak Jaya, New Guinea, 16,503 ft.

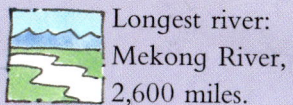 Longest river: Mekong River, 2,600 miles.

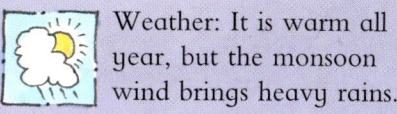 Weather: It is warm all year, but the monsoon wind brings heavy rains.

Many islanders live by fishing. Their boats are like canoes with small sails.

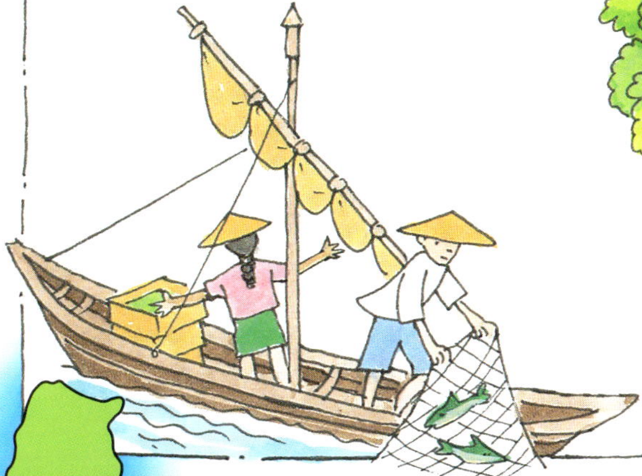

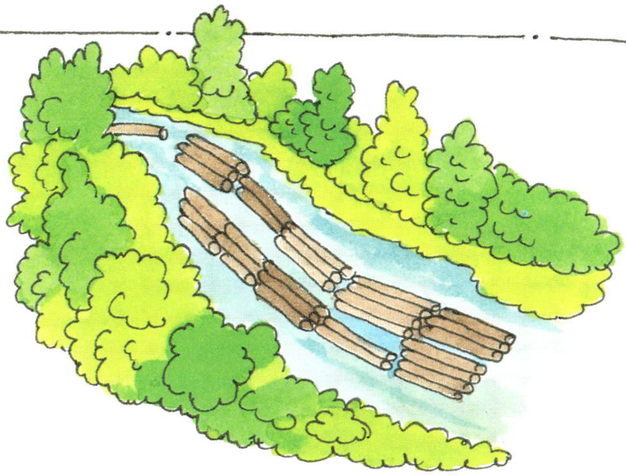

Timber is floated down rivers from forests to the sawmills.

Farmers grow many crops such as rice, maize, tea, coffee, and spices.

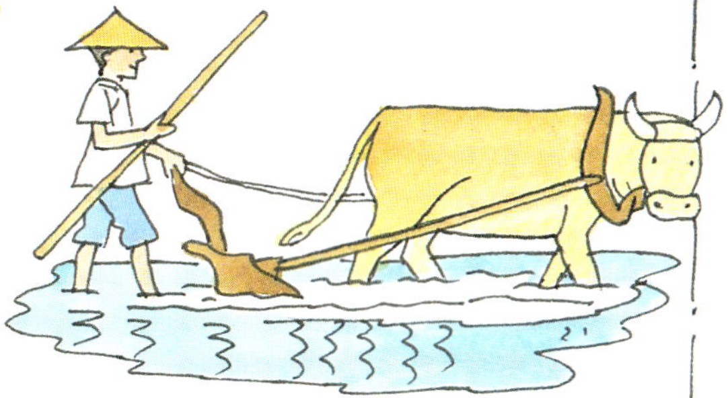

Luzon
MANILA
Pacific Ocean

Hundreds of languages are spoken in Southeast Asia and many different religions are practiced.

PHILIPPINES

Mindanao
Davao

There are over 7,000 islands in the Philippines.

Wooden house on stilts

Papua New Guinea is larger than California.

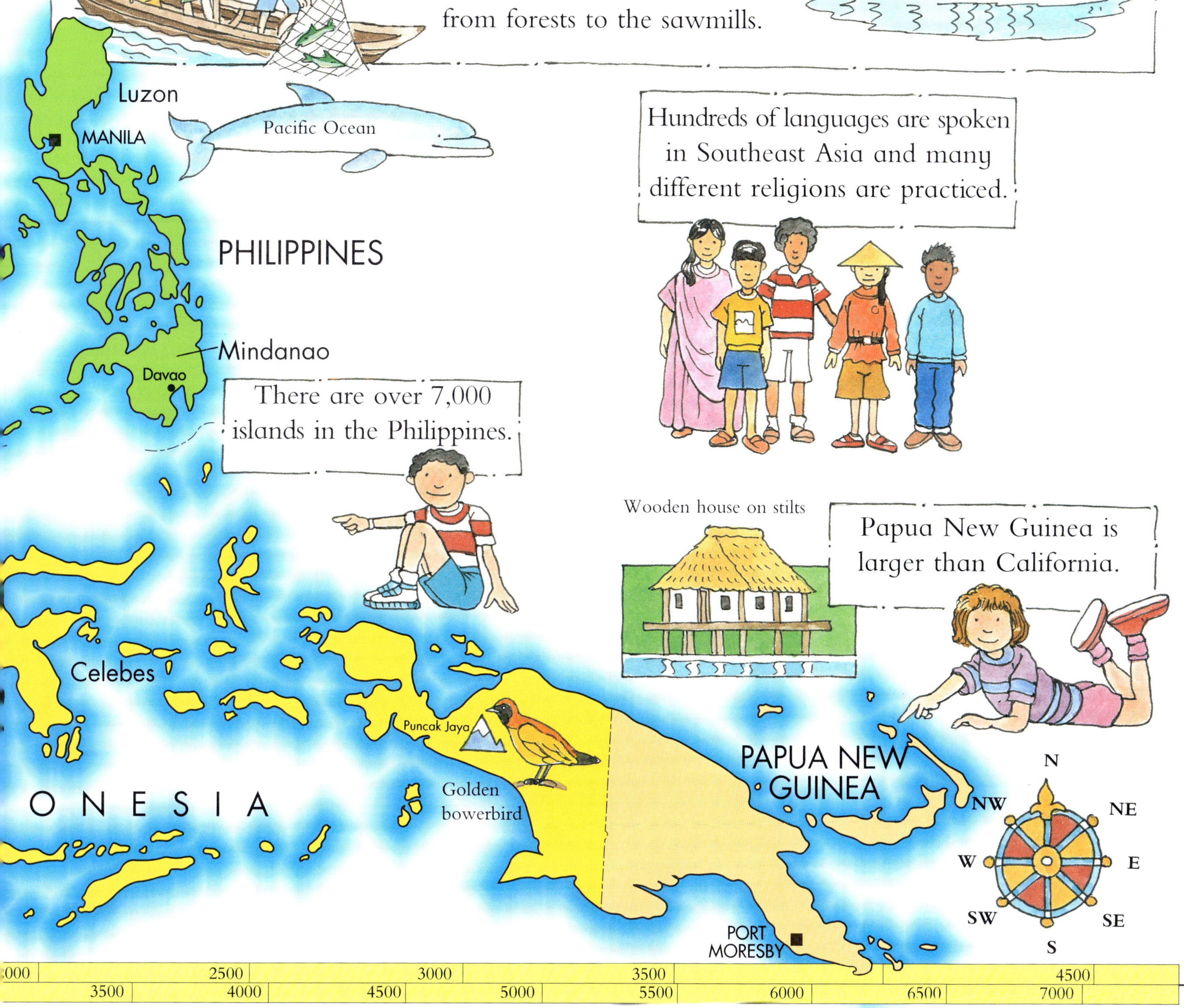

Celebes

Puncak Jaya
Golden bowerbird

ONESIA

PAPUA NEW GUINEA

PORT MORESBY

East Asia

More people live in China than in any other country in the world.

Japan is made up of four large islands and thousands of small ones.

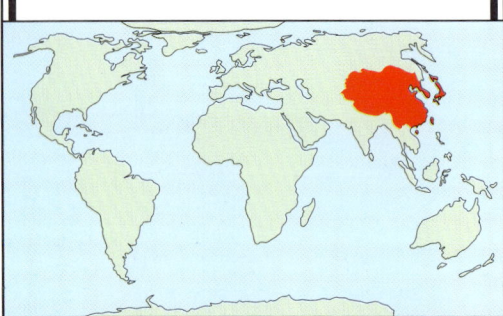

Mongolians are well known as expert horse riders.

The Great Wall of China was built to keep out enemies. It is 2,000 years old.

China's famous pottery and silk

Yak

Tibetan Plateau

CHINA

Altai Mountains

Urumchi

River Brahmaputra

Lhasa

River Mekong

Himalayas

Mount Everest

Mount Everest is on the border of China and Nepal.

China is the world's largest rice producer. The rice is planted in flooded fields known as paddies.

Miles		250	500		1000	
Kilometers	250	500	1000	1500		2000

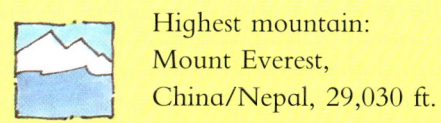 Highest mountain: Mount Everest, China/Nepal, 29,030 ft.

 Longest river: Chang Jiang, China, 3,436 miles.

 Weather: The north has wet summers and dry winters. The south is hot all year.

Mongolian herders live in tents called yurts, made from felt and cloth.

ULAN BATOR

MONGOLIA

Gobi Desert

Gunpowder was first used in China.

Harbin

Shenyang

Great Wall of China

BEIJING

Taiyuan

Huang He

Xi'an

Chengdu

Chang Jiang (River Yangtze)

Nanjing

Shanghai

A Chinese houseboat

Giant panda

Guangzhou

TAIPEI

TAIWAN

HONG KONG
MACAO

Pacific Ocean

Ch'ongjin

NORTH KOREA

PYONGYANG

Sea of Japan

SEOUL

SOUTH KOREA

Pusan

Kitakyushu

Sapporo

Osaka

TOKYO

JAPAN

There are ornate temples and shrines in Japan.

Japan makes many electronic goods, such as computers, radios, and televisions.

N
NW   NE
W   E
SW   SE
S

Australia and New Zealand

A large part of Australia is very dry and barren. This is known as the "outback."

New Zealand is 950 miles southeast of Australia.

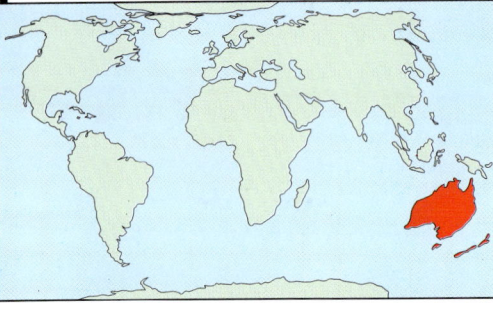

Australia has the world's largest wool industry. More sheep than people live here!

- Darwin

Kangaroo

Platypus

AUSTRALI

Hamersley Range

Emu

Macdonnel Ranges

Alice Spring

Giant Australian earthworm

1850s Gold Rush

Great Victoria Desert

Estuarine crocodile

• Perth

Indian Ocean

Aboriginal painting

Australia's native people are called Aborigines. They were the country's only inhabitants until about 200 years ago.

MILES	250	500		1000	
KILOMETERS		500	1000	1500	2000

 Highest mountain: Mount Cook, New Zealand, 12,350 ft.

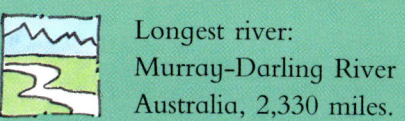 Longest river: Murray-Darling River Australia, 2,330 miles.

 Weather: Most of Australia is dry and hot. It is wet in the eastern mountains and in New Zealand.

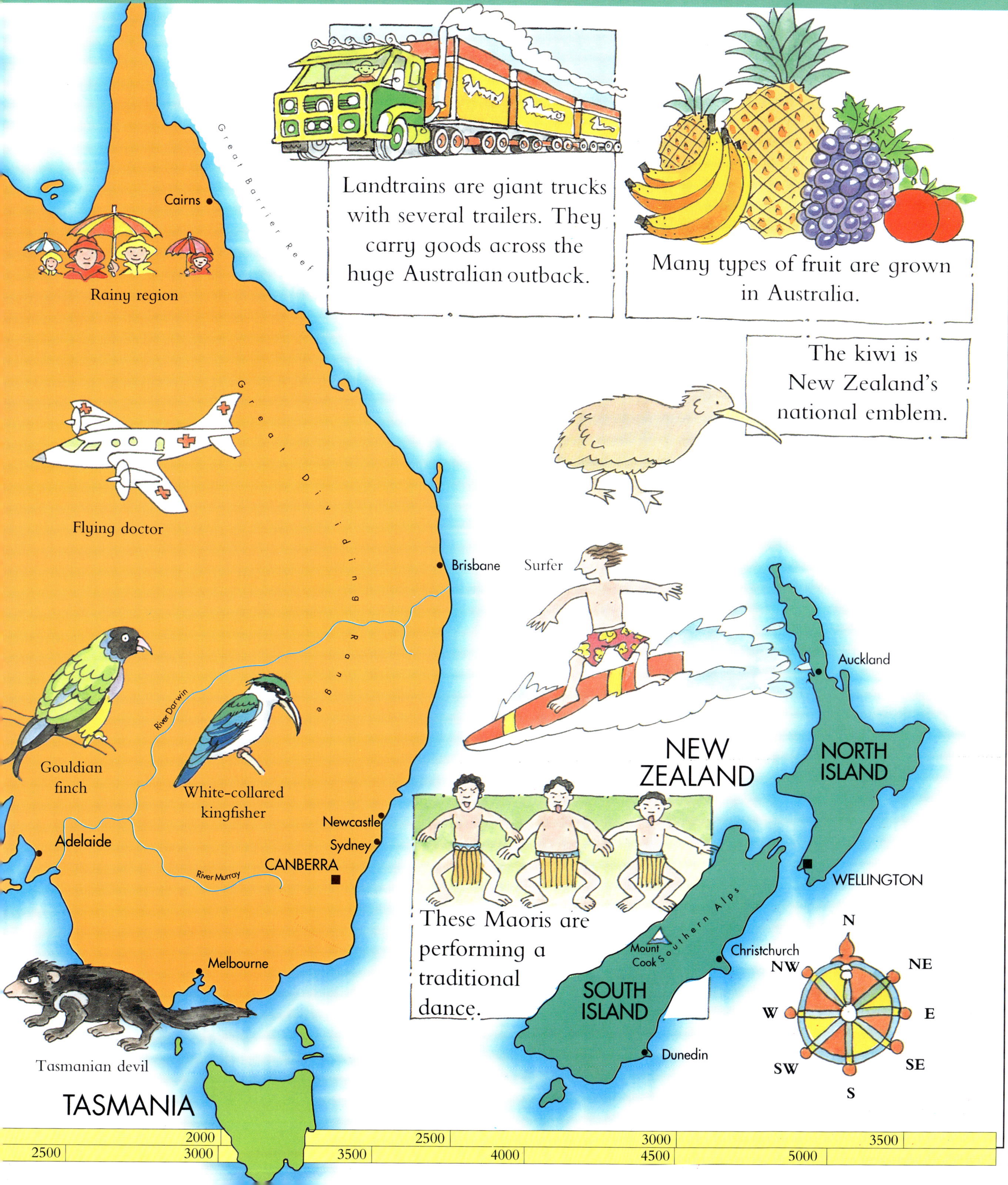

Landtrains are giant trucks with several trailers. They carry goods across the huge Australian outback.

Many types of fruit are grown in Australia.

The kiwi is New Zealand's national emblem.

Rainy region

Cairns

Great Barrier Reef

Flying doctor

Great Dividing Range

River Darwin

Gouldian finch

White-collared kingfisher

Adelaide

River Murray

Newcastle

Sydney

CANBERRA

Brisbane

Surfer

NEW ZEALAND

NORTH ISLAND

Auckland

WELLINGTON

These Maoris are performing a traditional dance.

Mount Cook

Southern Alps

Christchurch

SOUTH ISLAND

Dunedin

Melbourne

Tasmanian devil

TASMANIA

N NE E SE S SW W NW

Arctic

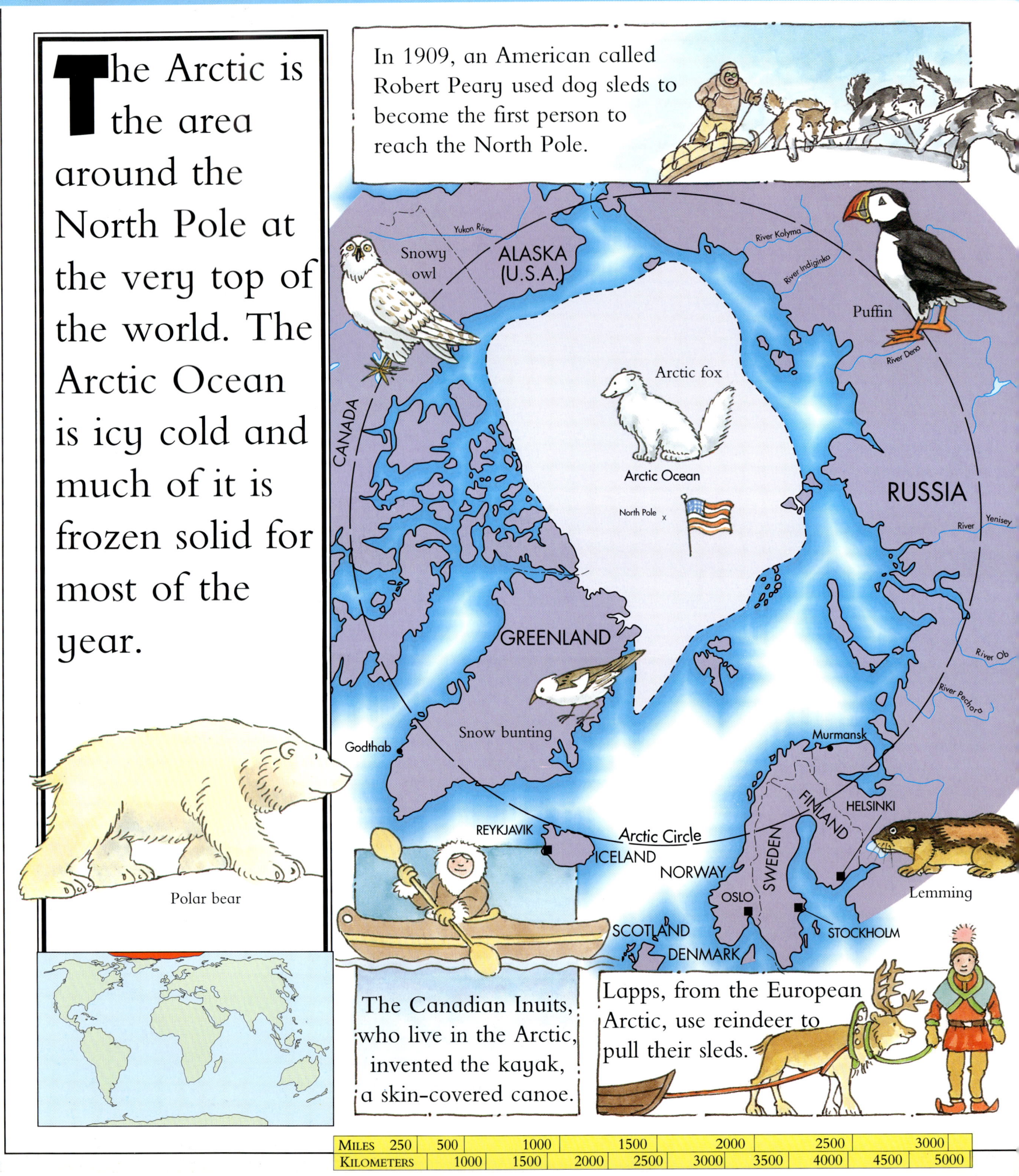

The Arctic is the area around the North Pole at the very top of the world. The Arctic Ocean is icy cold and much of it is frozen solid for most of the year.

In 1909, an American called Robert Peary used dog sleds to become the first person to reach the North Pole.

The Canadian Inuits, who live in the Arctic, invented the kayak, a skin-covered canoe.

Lapps, from the European Arctic, use reindeer to pull their sleds.

MILES	250	500	1000	1500	2000	2500	3000
KILOMETERS		1000	1500	2000	2500	3000	3500	4000	4500	5000

Antarctica

Antarctica is at the bottom of the world. Unlike the frozen Arctic Ocean, Antarctica is actually ice-covered land. In some places the ice is 15,670 feet thick.

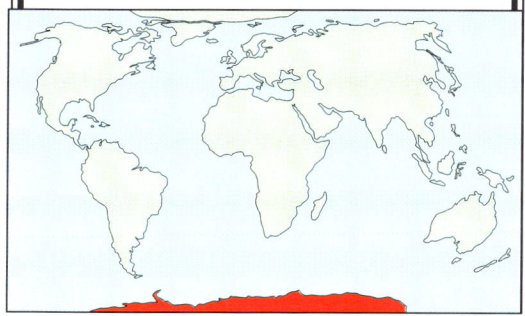

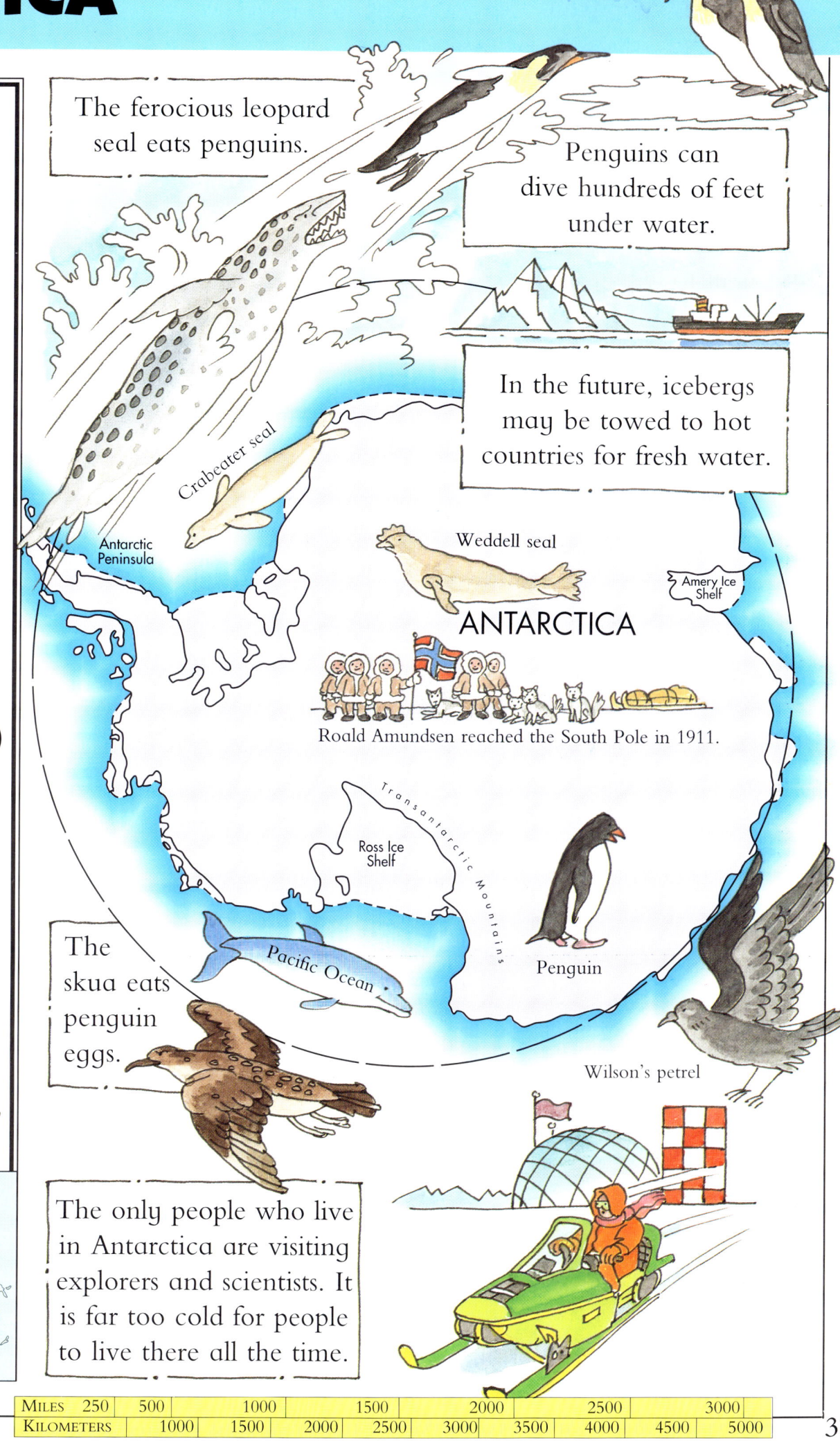

The ferocious leopard seal eats penguins.

Penguins can dive hundreds of feet under water.

In the future, icebergs may be towed to hot countries for fresh water.

Crabeater seal

Antarctic Peninsula

Weddell seal

Amery Ice Shelf

ANTARCTICA

Roald Amundsen reached the South Pole in 1911.

Transantarctic Mountains

Ross Ice Shelf

Pacific Ocean

Penguin

The skua eats penguin eggs.

Wilson's petrel

The only people who live in Antarctica are visiting explorers and scientists. It is far too cold for people to live there all the time.

MILES	250	500		1000		1500		2000		2500		3000	
KILOMETERS			1000	1500	2000	2500	3000	3500	4000	4500	5000		

World Facts

Coldest

Antarctica is the coldest place in the world. It can be as cold as −55°F.

Oceans

More than seven-tenths of the world is covered by water. The largest ocean is the Pacific. It covers almost one-third of the Earth's surface—64,185,611 sq. miles.

Earthquakes

Some parts of the world have more earthquakes than others. They are near faults, where pieces of land rub against each other, making the ground tremble. San Francisco, U.S.A., is built near a fault and suffers from earthquakes.

Size of Continents

Asia	16,820,447 sq. miles
Africa	11,684,158 sq. miles
North America	9,034,740 sq. miles
South America	6,874,897 sq. miles
Antarctica	5,405,400 sq. miles
Europe	4,062,158 sq. miles
Australia	2,967,565 sq. miles

Wettest

Mawsynram, in India, is the wettest place in the world. Every year it has over 46 inches of rain.

Driest

In 1971, part of the Atacama Desert, in Peru, had its first rainfall in 400 years.

DESERTS

The Sahara in North Africa is the largest desert in the world. It covers an area bigger than Australia!

MOUNTAINS

The highest mountain in the world is Mount Everest on the China/Nepal border. It is 29,030 feet high.

LARGEST COUNTRIES

Russia	6,592,812 sq. miles
Canada	3,851,787 sq. miles
China	3,693,418 sq. miles
U.S.A.	3,618,766 sq. miles
Brazil	3,286,470 sq. miles

HOTTEST

One of the hottest places in the world is Death Valley in California, U.S.A. Temperatures there can climb higher than 129°F.

VALLEYS

The Marianas Trench is a valley at the bottom of the Pacific Ocean. With a depth of 39,841 feet, it is the deepest valley in the world.

VOLCANOES

There are 200 active volcanoes in Indonesia.

INDEX

A

Afghanistan 27, 28
Africa 5, 24-5
Albania 21
Algeria 24
Andorra 20
Angola 25
Antarctica 5, 37
Arctic 36
Argentina 19
Armenia 22
Asia 5, 28-33
Australia 5, 34-5
Austria 21
Azerbaijan 22

B

Bahamas 17
Bahrain 27
Bangladesh 29
Belarus 21, 22
Belgium 20
Belize 15, 17
Benin 24
Bermuda 17
Bhutan 29
Bolivia 19
Bosnia and Herzegovina 21
Botswana 25
Brazil 19
Brunei 30
Bulgaria 21
Burma 29, 30
Burundi 25
Burkina Faso 24

C

Cambodia 30
Cameroon 24
Canada 14, 17, 36
Central African Republic 25
Central America 15
Chad 25
Chile 19
China 32-3
C.I.S. 22-3
Colombia 19
Congo 24
Costa Rica 15, 17
Croatia 21
Cuba 17
Cyprus 26
Czech Republic 21

D

Denmark 21, 36
Djibouti 25

E

Ecuador 19
Egypt 25
El Salvador 15, 17
England 20
Equatorial Guinea 24
Estonia 21, 22
Ethiopia 25
Eritrea 25
Europe 5, 20-1

F

Falkland Islands 19
Finland 21, 36
France 20
French Guiana 19

G

Gabon 24
Gambia, The 24
Georgia 21, 22
Germany 21
Ghana 24
Greece 21
Greenland 36
Guatemala 15, 17
Guinea 24
Guinea-Bissau 24
Guyana 19

H

Honduras 15, 17
Hong Kong 33
Hungary 21

I

Iceland 36
India 28-9
Indonesia 30-1
Iran 27
Iraq 26-7
Ireland, Northern 20
Ireland, Republic of 20
Israel 26
Italy 21
Ivory Coast 24

J

Jamaica 17
Japan 33
Jordan 26

K

Kazakhstan 22
Kenya 25
Korea, North 33
Korea, South 33
Kuwait 27
Kyrgyzstan 22

L

Laos 30
Latvia 21, 22
Lebanon 26
Lesotho 25
Liberia 24
Libya 25
Liechtenstein 21
Lithuania 21, 22
Luxembourg 21

M

Macedonia 21
Madagascar 25
Malawi 25
Malaysia 30
Mali 24
Malta 21
Mauritania 24
Mexico 15, 17
Moldova 22
Mongolia 32-3
Morocco 24
Mozambique 25
Myanmar, Union of 29, 30

N

Namibia 25
Nepal 29
Netherlands 21
New Zealand 35
Nicaragua 15, 17
Niger 24
Nigeria 24
North America 4, 16-7
Norway 21, 36

O

Oman 27

P

Pakistan 28
Panama 15, 17, 19
Papua New Guinea 31
Paraguay 19
Peru 19
Philippines 30-1
Poland 21
Portugal 20

Q

Qatar 27

R

Romania 21
Russia 21, 22-3, 36
Rwanda 25

S

Saudi Arabia 26-7
Scotland 20
Senegal 24
Sierra Leone 24
Singapore 30
Slovak Republic 21
Slovenia 21
Somalia 25
South Africa 25
South America 4, 18-19
Spain 20
Sri Lanka 29
Sudan 25
Suriname 19
Swaziland 25
Sweden 21, 36
Switzerland 21
Syria 26

T

Taiwan 33
Tajikistan 22
Tanzania 25
Thailand 30
Togo 24
Tunisia 24
Turkey 21, 26
Turkmenistan 22

U

Uganda 25
Ukraine 21, 22
United Arab Emirates 27
United Kingdom 20
Uruguay 19
U.S.A. 12-3, 17
Uzbekistan 22

V

Venezuela 19
Vietnam 30

W

Wales 20
Western Sahara 24

Y

Yemen, Republic of 27
Yugoslavia 21

Z

Zaire 25
Zambia 25
Zimbabwe 25

PART 2

YOUNG LEARNER'S ENCYCLOPEDIA

ALL ABOUT THE WORLD YOU LIVE IN

CONTENTS

Our World	42	New Technology	62
The Earth	44	Your Body	64
The Sea	46	Food	66
Weather	48	Clothes	68
Plants	50	Sports	70
Animals	52	Homes	72
Prehistoric Times	54	Occupations	74
Ancient Times	56	Transport	76
Explorers	58	Space	78
Inventions	60	Index	80

Our World

Encyclopedias tell you all about the world we live in. In this one, you will find a different topic each time you turn a page. The index shows you exactly where you can find information.

A century of discovery

In the past hundred years more changes have taken place in our world than at any other time in history. Explorers have reached the icy North and South poles, explored the depths of the oceans, and traveled into space. Scientists have found wonderful uses for electricity and invented the microchip. Archaeologists have discovered how people lived in the past. Who knows what the next hundred years will bring?

A world of information

Before printing was invented, most people knew very little about the world outside their own village. Printed books made knowledge available to all. Now radio, television, and computers bring us information at the press of a button. Jet aircraft carry us to the other side of the world in less than a day.

Modern communications have made our world seem a smaller place.

Strange but True

Use the dictionary to look up words. The atlas shows you where places are.

★ Every minute of every day 100 acres of tropical rainforest is destroyed. At this rate there will be no rainforest left in 40 years.

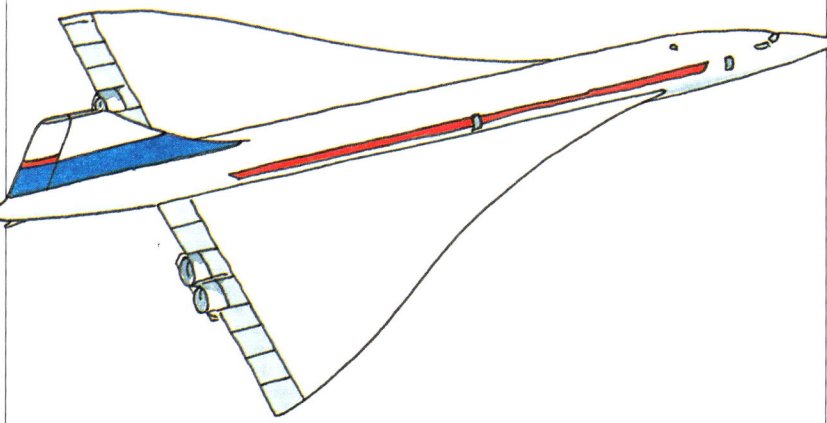

★ The Concorde flies from London to New York in just under four hours. Because of the time difference, you arrive in New York an hour before you left London.

Tomorrow's world

We depend on the land to produce enough food for everyone. We want to breathe clean air and drink pure water. Fossil fuels, such as oil and gas, will not last forever. As we learn more about our world, we understand how important it is to take care of it.

World records

Antarctica contains 99 per cent of the world's ice.

The Pacific Ocean is almost as big as all the other oceans put together.

The highest mountain is Mount Everest. It is 29,030 feet high. Clouds often hide the peak.

In comparison to some of the other planets in the Solar System, our world is quite small. If you walked fast without stopping, you could walk right round the Equator in 250 days. It would take 10 times longer to walk around Saturn.

The Earth

The planet Earth is one of nine planets that circle the Sun.

None of the other planets can support life. Only Earth has an atmosphere to breathe, water to drink, and plants and animals.

Inside the Earth

If you could cut the Earth in half, you would see that it is made up of layers. At the center is a heavy, hot core of molten metal. Then there is a mantle of rock. The mantle is cooler than the core, and like thick syrup. The outer crust is the layer on which we live. Proportionately it is as thin as a coat of paint on a basketball.

Earthquakes and Volcanoes

The thin crust of Earth's surface floats on the mantle. The crust moves constantly. Over time parts of it called plates slide or grate against each other

When a volcano erupts, hot molten rock and gases force their way up from below the crust. The red-hot rock spews into the air. Molten rock flowing down from a volcano is called lava.

Mountains and rivers

Sometimes the plates of Earth's crust collide. Over time, great mountain ranges are created. As rain falls it runs down mountains and hillsides. Streams and rivers form. Some carve great canyons in the land. Rivers flow into lakes and the sea.

Rocks, mining, and oil

Rocks in the Earth's crust are used to make buildings and roads. Some rocks contain metal ores. These are mined to make metals such as iron and aluminum. Other rocks trap underground lakes of oil and natural gas.

Drilling deep into the Earth's crust brings the oil and gas to the surface.

Very hot and very cold

Deserts are dry because very little rain falls. During the days when it is very hot, the animals that live there have to find places to shelter from the sun. Camels, which live in some deserts, can travel great distances without drinking water. Deserts can be cold at night.

At the North and South poles there is always snow and ice. Polar bears have thick fur coats to protect them.

STRANGE BUT TRUE

* In Asia, people used to believe that the world was supported by a tortoise that lived on the backs of four elephants.

* In 1968, three U.S. astronauts became the first people to see the shape of the Earth with their own eyes. Before then, people had only seen parts of the Earth.

* At the Equator, the Earth rotates at 1,000 m.p.h. Without the force of gravity, you would fly out into space.

The Sea

From space, the world looks blue. This is because nearly three-quarters of its surface is covered with water. The four great oceans of the world are the Atlantic Ocean, the Pacific Ocean, the Indian Ocean, and the Arctic Ocean.

Harvesting the seas

Great numbers of fish feed and breed in the shallow water that surrounds the continents. This is where fishing fleets do most of their fishing.

Low tide, high tide

Tides come in and go out twice a day at the seaside. They are caused by the Moon attracting the sea towards it.

The sea comes much further up the beach at high tide. The highest tides are in spring and fall.

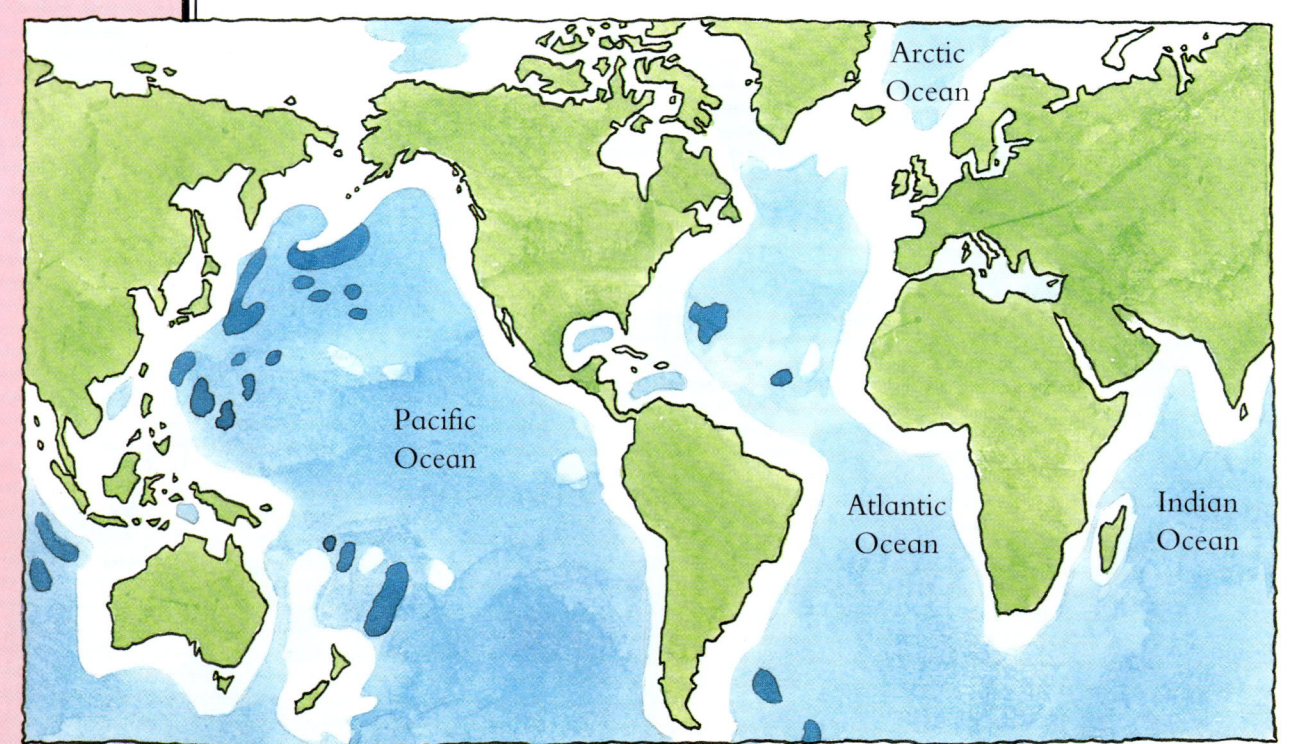

Giants of the ocean

Whales are the largest mammals. The blue whale, which is shown below, weighs more than 100 tons and is about 100 feet long. Killer whales hunt in packs and attack other whales as well as dolphins, seals, and penguins. Squid, which can weigh 10 tons and measure 56 feet, are the largest animals without a backbone.

Coral islands

Coral is the chalky skeleton of a tiny animal called a coral polyp. Each new polyp grows from the side of its parent. More and more coral builds up in the shallow warm sea water near islands. A large coral reef takes hundreds of years to grow. It provides a home for many sea creatures.

There is so much salt in the Dead Sea that you can sit up as you float.

Strange but true

★ The Australian Great Barrier Reef is 1,260 miles long. It can be seen from the Moon.

★ Inuit use sea ice as a source of fresh water for drinking. When the surface of the sea freezes, the salt is left behind in the water.

Weather

Weather is part of our daily lives. It affects the way we dress, what we eat, and how we spend our time.

In some parts of the world the weather stays much the same day after day. In others it is always changing.

The Atmosphere

Weather is caused by changes in the atmosphere, the blanket of air above the Earth. Clouds, rain, wind, and heat waves are all produced in the bottom layer of the atmosphere, called the troposphere. Jet aircraft often fly above the clouds where the air is calmer.

The Wind

Weather changes are blown around the world by winds. Winds are formed when the Sun heats up some parts of the Earth more strongly than others, and the difference in heat makes the air move. Hurricanes and tornadoes form in warm, damp air when winds hurl into each other from opposite directions.

The Water Cycle

The Sun heats the sea and turns some of it into water vapor, which rises into the sky to make a cloud. The wind blows the cloud across the sky. When the cloud reaches warm land it rises and meets cold air. This cools the cloud and turns the vapor into water again. The drops fall as rain, which trickles down the mountains and forms rivers. Water also filters through to the water table.

Water vapor

Water table

SNOW

If the air in a cloud is below freezing, some of the water vapor freezes into ice crystals. These crystals stick together to make snowflakes. Every snowflake has six points, but each one has a different shape.

STRANGE BUT TRUE

* You can work out how far away a storm is by counting the seconds between the lightning and thunder. Five seconds equals 1 mile.

* In the U.S., hurricanes are given people's names in alphabetical order.

CLIMATE

Climate is the usual weather of a place over a long period of time. The weather may change from day to day, but the climate stays the same. A place's climate depends on how close it is to the Equator. Countries near the Equator get more of the Sun's rays and usually have a hotter climate than places further north or south.

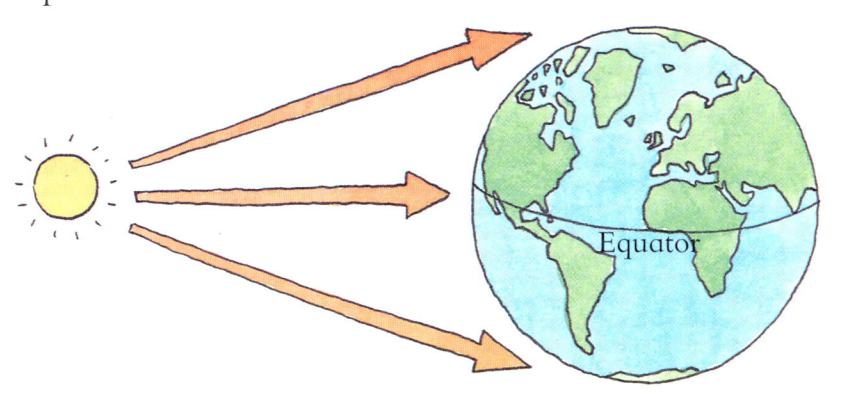

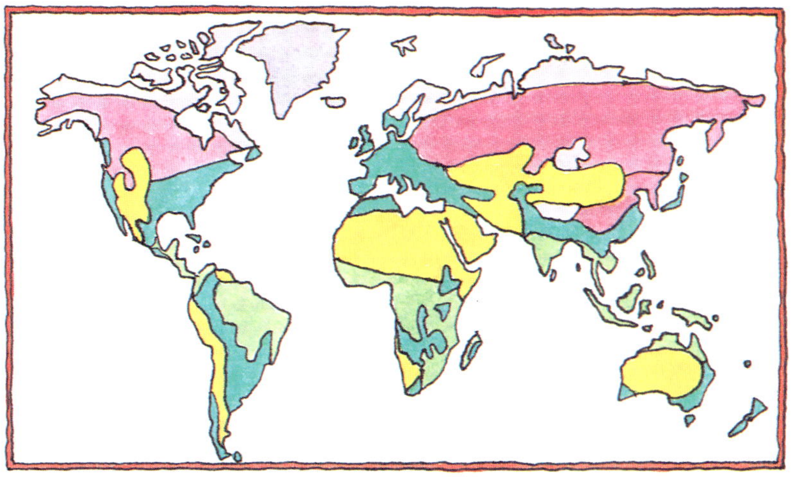

FORECASTING

Weather forecasters collect information and take measurements to provide a picture of how the atmosphere is behaving.

Red sky at night, sailor's delight. Red sky in the morning, sailor's warning.

STORMY WEATHER

Thunderstorms are caused by electricity in the air. The electrical charges that build up inside rain clouds make flashes of lightning. The worst type of storm is a hurricane, which can cause a lot of damage. Information sent back to Earth from satellites can help warn of a developing storm.

- **Polar** Cold and dry. Always icy at the poles.
- **Cold forests** Long snowy winters and short warm summers.
- **Temperate** Not too hot nor too cold. Rain all year.
- **Dry** Deserts very hot and dry all year, with hardly any rain. Mountain areas dry and cold.
- **Tropical** Hot all year. Wet and dry seasons on the grasslands. Rainy all year in the forests. Hurricanes start in the tropics.

Plants

Plants make the food that animals eat. Most plants produce flowers and seeds so they can reproduce. They are divided up into groups by the things they have in common. These groups are called families.

Garden flowers, vegetables, fruits, and grasses are all flowering plants. Many trees and shrubs also have flowers.

Parts of a flowering plant

The flower attracts insects with its color and scent. Insects carry pollen from the male part of the flower, called the stamen, to the female part, the pistil.

When a flower has been pollinated, it produces seeds from which new plants sprout and grow.

The leaves use sunlight to make food from air and water. This is called photosynthesis.

The stem carries food and water around the plant.

The roots hold the plant firmly in the ground. They suck in water and minerals from the soil.

Trapping the Sun's energy

Every living thing needs energy to keep it alive. Green plants trap the Sun's energy and make it into food. The energy in plant food passes on to the animals that eat the plants.

The air we breathe

Plants also provide the oxygen that we need to breathe. While they are making their food, plants take in the carbon dioxide gas that people and animals breathe out, and give off oxygen instead.

Evergreen trees

Trees that do not lose their leaves in the fall are called evergreens. Evergreens lose their leaves throughout the year, but are continually growing new ones.

Deciduous trees

Many of the trees found in cool countries lose their leaves in the fall. The leaves change color, then drop off and rot on the ground. Trees that lose their leaves in this way are called deciduous.

Tropical rainforests

Tropical rainforests are very hot and there is heavy rain most days. Trees quickly grow very tall. Rainforests are home to many different animals and birds, and produce 50% of the world's oxygen supply. In some parts of the world they are being destroyed. Many valuable plants are disappearing.

Plants without flowers

Algae are simple plants without flowers. The best known algae are seaweeds.

A fungus cannot make food for itself. It takes food from other living things, or from dead wood and leaves. Toadstools and mushrooms are fungi. Their caps produce spores that grow into new plants.

Mosses grow in damp places. They produce capsules on thin stalks. The capsules release powdery spores that grow into new plants.

Ferns have leaves, or fronds, which grow up from an underground stem. Spores are carried under the fronds.

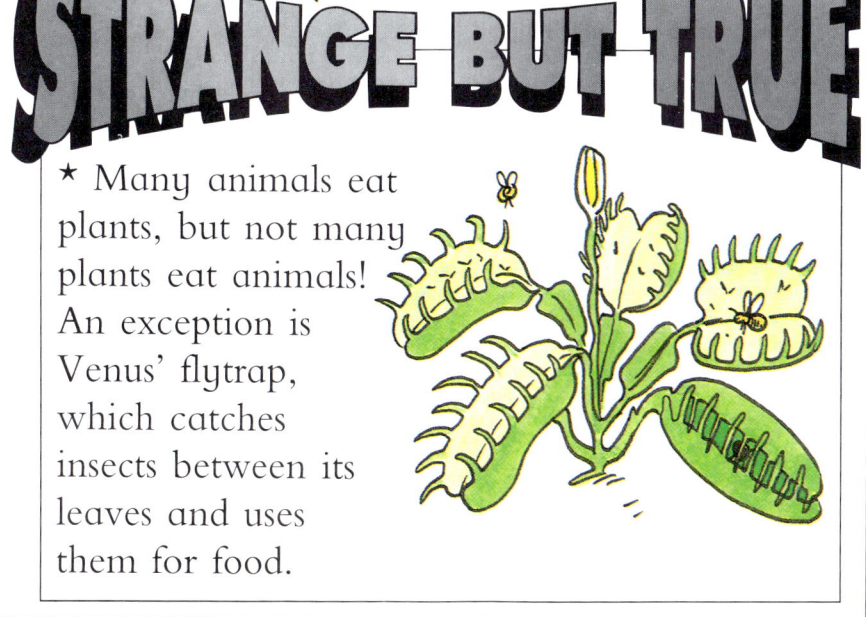

STRANGE BUT TRUE

★ Many animals eat plants, but not many plants eat animals! An exception is Venus' flytrap, which catches insects between its leaves and uses them for food.

ANIMALS

An animal is any living thing that is not a plant. Nobody knows how many different animals there are. New kinds are discovered every year. Animals are divided into groups by their characteristics. Mammals were the last group to appear on Earth.

Fish

Fish are coldblooded animals that live in the water. Fish have backbones and are called vertebrates. They swim by moving their tails from side to side. Fish breathe through gills on each side of the head. Most fish lay eggs, but some give birth to live young.

Amphibians

Amphibians can live either in the water or on land. Like fish, amphibians are coldblooded animals with backbones. They lay eggs in a layer of jelly which protects them.

Reptiles

A reptile is a coldblooded animal that moves on its belly or its very short legs. For millions of years reptiles were the most numerous animals in the world. Now the only kinds left are tortoises and turtles, crocodiles and alligators, lizards, and snakes. Reptiles, like all coldblooded animals, get their warmth from the heat of the Sun.

The ancestors of modern fish appeared on Earth over 500 million years ago.

Frog eggs

Life cycle of a frog

Growing tadpoles

BIRDS

Birds are warmblooded animals. Some people believe they are descended from dinosaurs. Birds have feathers and wings. They have hollow bones so that they are light in the air, and strong breast muscles for flapping their wings. But some birds, like ostriches, cannot fly. Birds build nests, in which they lay eggs and raise their young.

STRANGE BUT TRUE

★ The tuatara has survived for 150 million years. This strange reptile lives on islands off the coast of New Zealand.

★ The echidna and the platypus are mammals, but they lay eggs.

INSECTS

Insects are invertebrates, animals without backbones. Instead of skeletons, their bodies are held together by a hard outer shell. All insects have three pairs of legs. Their bodies are divided into three parts: head, thorax, and abdomen. Some insects (such as bees, which pollinate plants) are helpful to humans; others, like the mosquito, are considered pests.

Life cycle of a butterfly

Egg
Caterpillar
Pupa

MAMMALS

Mammals have warm blood and a bony skeleton. Many have hair or fur on their bodies to keep them warm. Most mammals give birth to live babies, which are fed with milk produced by the mother. Marsupials, such as kangaroos, are carried in their mother's pouch until they are fully developed. The most intelligent mammals are the primates. This family includes monkeys, apes, and humans.

A FOOD PYRAMID

In the African savanna, antelopes, wildebeest, and zebra feed on grass and leafy shrubs. These herbivores are prey for the meat-eaters, or carnivores.

Prehistoric Times

Most of the plants and animals that lived millions of years ago were quite different from those we know today. Scientists have discovered what they looked like by studying fossils preserved in rocks, and remains found in ice.

The first plants

About 350 million years ago, great forests covered the Earth. Most of the plants were giant sized. When the plants died they fell into the swampy ground. Over millions of years they became buried under more dead trees and the plants turned into coal.

The first animals

The first living things existed over 1.5 billion years ago. They were simple creatures that lived in the sea. Fish appeared 1 billion years later. They were followed by amphibians and then reptiles.

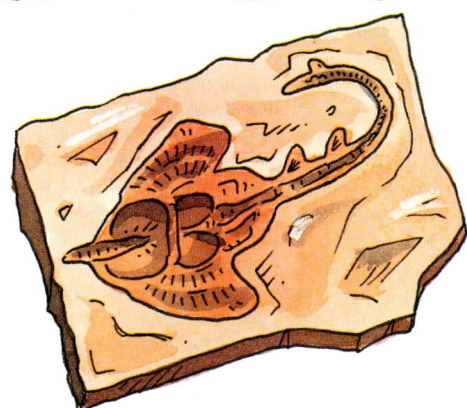

Trilobites and ammonites

Trilobites looked like large woodlice. The legs were used for walking on the bottom of the sea or for swimming. Ammonites had coiled shells. Some were very small and others grew to over 6 feet.

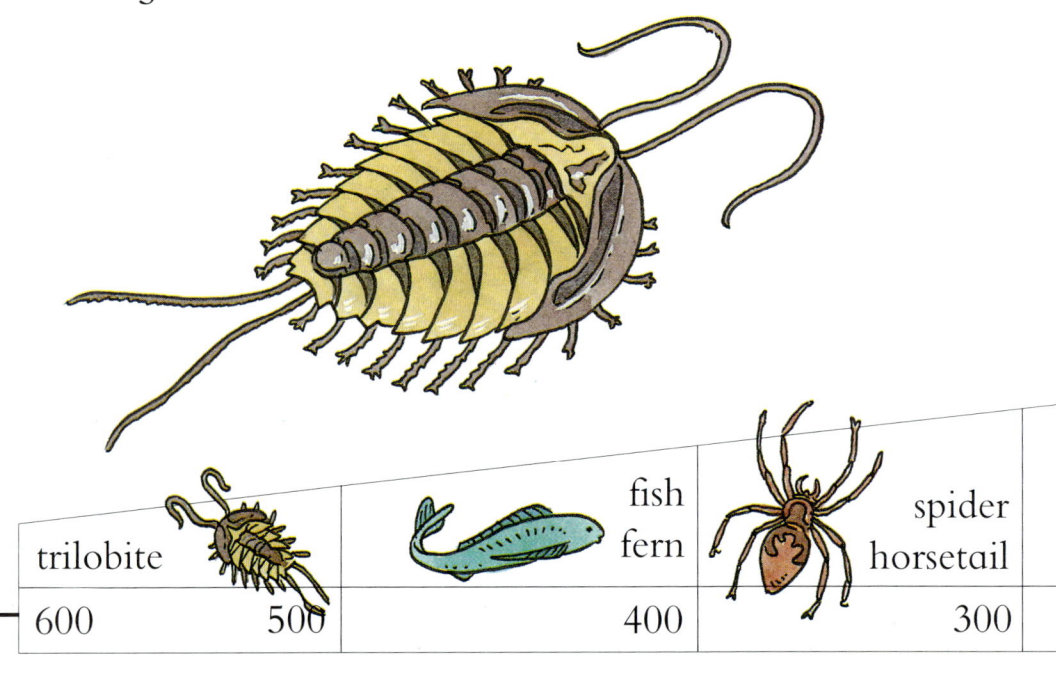

trilobite		fish fern	spider horsetail
600	500	400	300

Dinosaur means "terrible lizard."

STRANGE BUT TRUE

★ *Pachycephalosaurs* had very thick skulls. They were just like crash helmets. The males banged their heads together in fights.

FLYING REPTILES

The pterosaurs were flying reptiles. Their large wings stretched from a very long finger to the sides of the body and hind legs. The largest pterosaur was *pteranodon*, which had a wingspan of over 80 feet. The smallest was the size of a sparrow.

ARMOR-PLATING

Stegosaurus and *triceratops* were protected by armor. *Triceratops* had three horns and a bony frill across its neck. *Stegosaurus* had bony plates along its back.

DINOSAURS

Dinosaurs dominated the Earth for 140 million years. The largest were the four-footed vegetarian dinosaurs with long necks and tails. Other dinosaurs walked upright on their hind legs, with their very small front legs held off the ground. The largest of the two-legged dinosaurs was the fierce meat-eater, *Tyrannosaurus rex*.

WHY DID THEY DIE?

Dinosaurs and pterosaurs died out about 65 million years ago. What killed them remains one of the great puzzles of the past. Some scientists believe that the climate grew too cold for them to survive. Their place was taken by a different group of animals, the warmblooded mammals.

million years ago

ammonite cycad dimetrodon	diplodocus stegosaurus ichthyosaurus archaeopteryx	tyrannosaurus triceratops iguanadon pteranodon	*Australopithecus* (not quite a caveman) ape butterfly early horse mammoth
200	135	65	1.8

Ancient Times

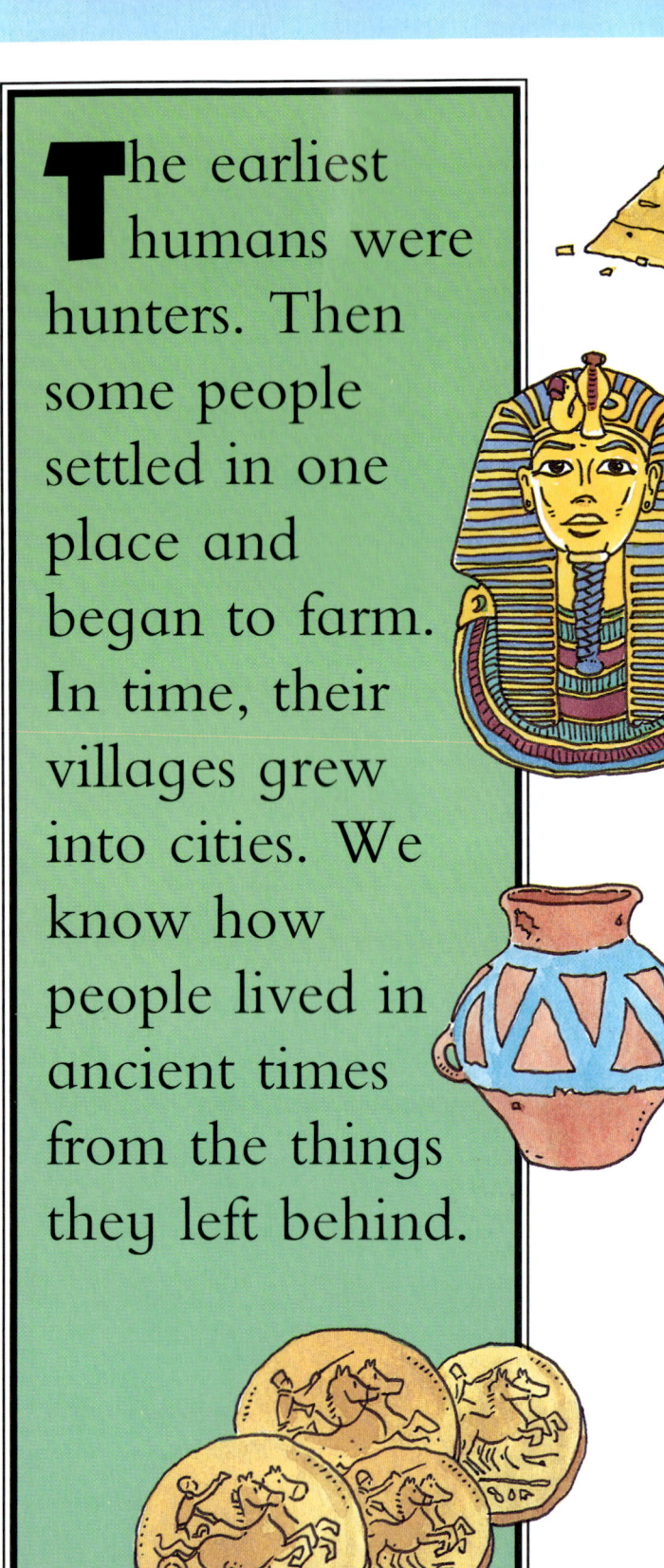

The earliest humans were hunters. Then some people settled in one place and began to farm. In time, their villages grew into cities. We know how people lived in ancient times from the things they left behind.

100,000 people toiled for 20 years to build the Great Pyramid!

The Egyptians

About 5,000 years ago people settled by the Nile River and learned how to grow grain in the fertile soil. They also became skilled artists, sculptors, and builders. The most splendid buildings were the pyramids, the tombs of the Pharaohs. The ancient Egyptians put in their tombs everything they thought they would need in the next world.

The Chinese

The first Chinese civilization grew up in the valley of the Hwang Ho River. By 1500 B.C. China had become a kingdom ruled by powerful families. The ancient Chinese knew how to cast bronze, weave silk, and make pots. They invented printing and gunpowder.

The Greeks

The Greeks loved art, the theater, poetry, and sport. One of the most powerful cities was Athens, which had beautiful buildings decorated with sculpture.

Even people sitting at the back of an open-air amphitheater could hear a pin drop.

THE ROMANS

The Romans had a strong army and built up a vast empire around the Mediterranean Sea. Rome, in Italy, was the capital. For a time Rome was ruled by a government of senators until, in 49 B.C., Julius Caesar made himself Emperor. The Romans were expert builders and engineers. Remains of their roads, villas, aqueducts, and baths can still be found in Europe today.

THE INCAS

The Incas ruled a great empire in South America from A.D. 1200-1500. Cities like Machu Picchu were built high in the Andes mountains. The Incas wove beautiful materials with brightly-colored designs and made gold jewelry and ornaments. In 1533 a Spanish army led by Pizarro, greedy for gold, conquered the Inca empire.

THE AZTECS

In 1345 a small tribe of hunters founded the city of Tenochtitlan on Lake Texcoco in Mexico. In less than 200 years they ruled an empire that stretched from coast to coast. The Aztecs were interested in astronomy and mathematics, and developed their own calendar. Great temples were built to honor their many gods.

HOW THEY WROTE

Ancient Egyptian writing is called hieroglyphics.

The characters used in Chinese writing developed from early picture-writing.

Our alphabet comes from the Roman letters of 2,500 years ago.

Aa Bb Cc Dd Ee

STRANGE BUT TRUE

★ The Great Pyramid at Giza is 450 feet high and built of 2,300,000 blocks of stone. The ancient Egyptians had no cranes, so they may have dragged the blocks using rollers and pulled the huge stones up a long ramp.

★ The Incas had no money or writing, but kept accurate accounts by making knots in pieces of string. These quipus were also used for sending messages.

3000	2000	1000	B.C | A.D. 0	1000	2000
Egyptians		Chinese Greeks Romans			Incas Aztecs

Explorers

Since ancient times, people have traveled and settled in different places. Many early explorers set out to find new lands and new people to trade with. Today nearly all of the world has been discovered and mapped by explorers who made dangerous voyages by sea, or journeys by land or air.

Vikings

The Vikings were sea warriors who sailed far in their magnificent longboats. From the 8th to the 11th century these Norsemen, or men from the North, terrorized Europe, taking slaves and stealing treasure from monasteries and churches. They were also settlers and explorers. One of them, Leif Eriksson, son of Erik the Red, crossed the Atlantic to a place he called Vinland. Remains of a Viking settlement in Newfoundland show that Vikings reached North America before other Europeans.

Marco Polo

Marco Polo was 17 years old when he traveled overland to China from Venice in the 13th century. He served the Chinese Emperor Kublai Khan for 17 years. On his return, 24 years later, he wrote about what he had seen. He told of fabulous riches as well as coal, paper money, gunpowder, and printing; things no one had ever seen or heard of in the West.

Finding the way

★ The magnetic needle of a compass points north.

★ A sextant helps you calculate where you are by measuring how high the Sun or a star appears to be at a particular time.

Traders and Adventurers

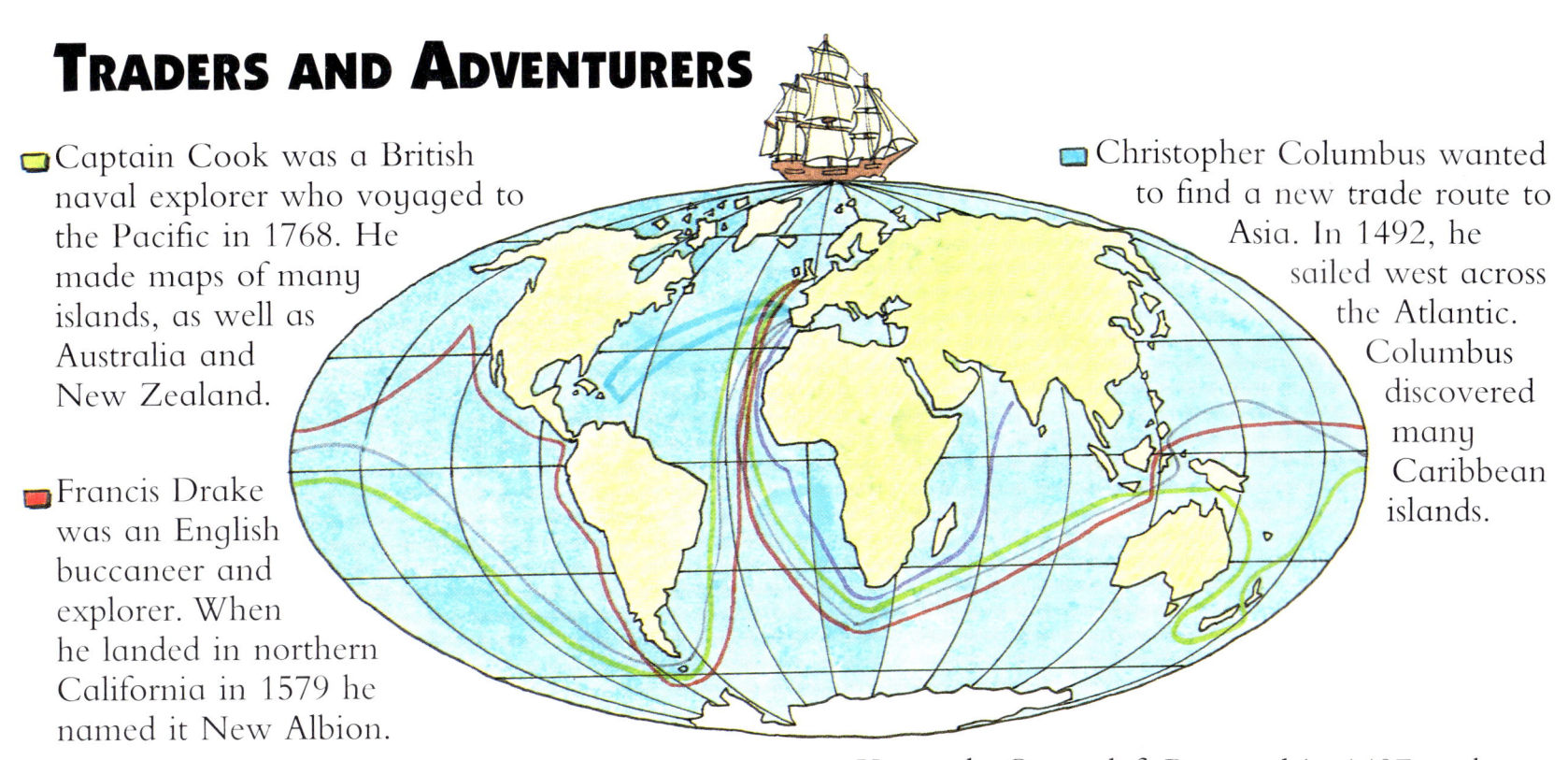

- Captain Cook was a British naval explorer who voyaged to the Pacific in 1768. He made maps of many islands, as well as Australia and New Zealand.

- Francis Drake was an English buccaneer and explorer. When he landed in northern California in 1579 he named it New Albion.

- Ferdinand Magellan, like Columbus, set out to find a new route to the East Indies. His 1519 expedition was the first to sail round the world.

- Christopher Columbus wanted to find a new trade route to Asia. In 1492, he sailed west across the Atlantic. Columbus discovered many Caribbean islands.

- Vasco da Gama left Portugal in 1497 and discovered the eastward route to India. He rounded the Cape of Good Hope at the southern tip of Africa and crossed the Indian Ocean.

Strange but True

* Early explorers believed the Earth was flat. They did not want to sail too far, in case they went over the edge!

The race for the poles

For a hundred years, explorers tried to reach the North Pole. The American Robert Edwin Peary reached it first in 1909. Huskies drew his sleds over the ice. There is no land at the North Pole, just the frozen Arctic Ocean. Racing for the South Pole in 1911, the Norwegian explorer Roald Amundsen beat the Englishman Robert Scott by one month. He also found the Northwest Passage and the magnetic pole.

INVENTIONS

In our century, the way we live has changed very fast. Not so long ago, most people lived the same way their grandparents did. A few key inventions, such as the wheel and electricity, have greatly changed the way we live.

THE WHEEL

No one knows who invented the wheel. People living in the Middle East used a horse-drawn war cart about 5,000 years ago. It had solid wheels made of wood. Later, chariots were made with spoked wheels. Now we depend on wheeled transport for nearly everything.

PRINTED BOOKS

The Chinese had printed books more than 1,000 years ago. But modern printing, using moveable letters made of metal, was invented by Johannes Gutenberg in 1447. Books made this way cost less and helped to make knowledge widely available.

Cotton

American Eli Whitney invented the cotton gin, a machine that separates cotton fibers from the seed, in 1792. The seeds must be removed before the fibers are spun into thread and woven. The separation was once done by hand.

Electricity

In 1831 Michael Faraday, an English scientist, invented the dynamo, a machine for making electricity. He also invented the transformer and the electric motor.

Strange but True

* The word electricity comes from *elektron*, the Greek word for amber, the fossilized resin of prehistoric trees. When it is rubbed, amber becomes charged with electricity.

* Thomas Alva Edison patented 1,300 inventions. One of his best known inventions was the phonograph, which he thought would be used in offices for dictation.

Electric light makes everything light as day.

The Steam Age

James Watt, a Scottish engineer, found a way to make steam engines work efficiently in 1763. His engines were used in factories and mines everywhere and started the Industrial Revolution in Britain. Forty years later another engineer, Richard Trevithick, invented the railway engine when he put a steam engine on wheels.

New Technology

Once the fastest way to send a message was by horse. Then railroads were invented and they carried the mail. Now new technologies have changed how we communicate. We send pictures, sound, and messages around the world by satellite, and into outer space.

Messages by wire

An American, Samuel Morse, invented a code of dots and dashes for the letters of the alphabet in 1837. The Morse code was used to communicate across long distances by sending electrical signals by wire. American Alexander Graham Bell invented the telephone. On June 5, 1875, he spoke the first words ever heard on the telephone to his assistant, Mr. Watson.

"Come here, Mr. Watson, I want to see you."

The coming of radio

Guglielmo Marconi transmitted the first radio signal across the Atlantic in 1901. It was the letter "S," three dots in Morse code. Now satellites above the Pacific, Atlantic, and Indian Oceans relay international telephone calls and transmit radio and television programs. They also link fax machines and computers together by radio.

TELEVISION BEGINS

Scotsman John Logie Baird made the first successful television transmission in 1925. The first regular television programs were made in England in 1936. Now, all over the world, television programs for entertainment, news, and sport are made. Television cameras guard stores against theft and the police use them to control traffic. Scientists use them to explore the bottom of the ocean and distant planets.

LASER LIGHT

A laser makes a narrow, powerful beam of light of one color. The first one was made by American Theodore H. Maiman in 1960. Today, lasers can be used by surgeons and dentists in place of the scalpel and drill. They are used in industry, in communications, and in every CD player.

COMPUTERS

The first computers were very big. They filled whole rooms. Then the transistor was invented in 1947, two days before Christmas, by Americans Walter Brattain, John Bardeen, and William Schockley. Now millions of transistors on a tiny piece of silicon, called a microchip, power today's desktop computers. They make many millions of calculations a second.

STRANGE BUT TRUE

★ The distance between the Earth and the Moon is about 238,857 miles. A laser has been used to measure it very accurately.

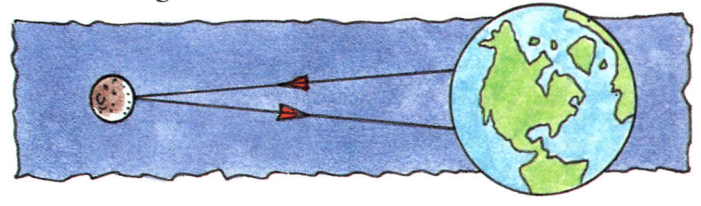

★ The science fiction writer, Arthur C. Clarke, predicted a system of artificial satellites in 1945, nearly 20 years before NASA launched the first communications satellite, Telstar.

63

Your Body

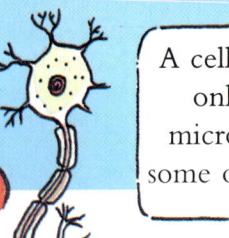

A cell is so small, you can only see it through a microscope. This is what some of your cells look like.

Underneath your skin, your body has many different parts. Each part has a different job to do. They all work to keep you alive. Your body needs the right amount of food, rest, and exercise to stay healthy and grow strong.

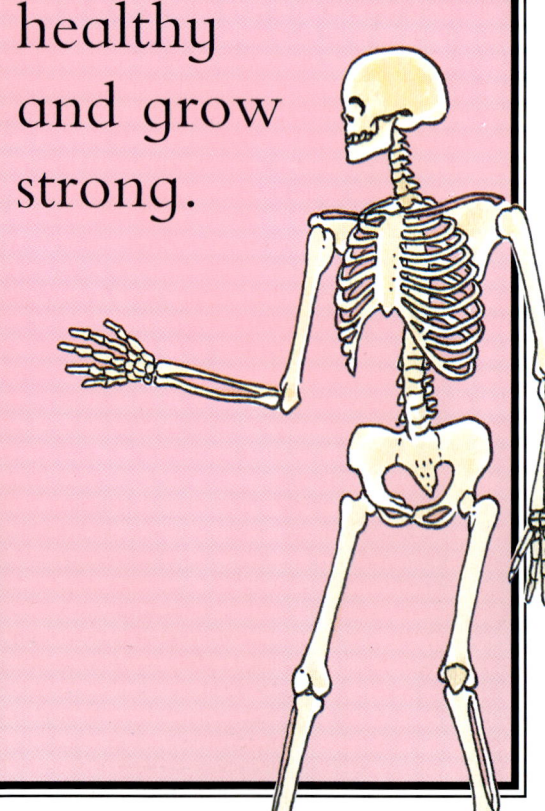

The Parts of Your Body

All living things are made up of cells. The parts of your body are made up of millions of tiny cells of many different kinds. Each kind of cell has a special job to do. Your blood carries to all the cells the food and oxygen that they need to live.

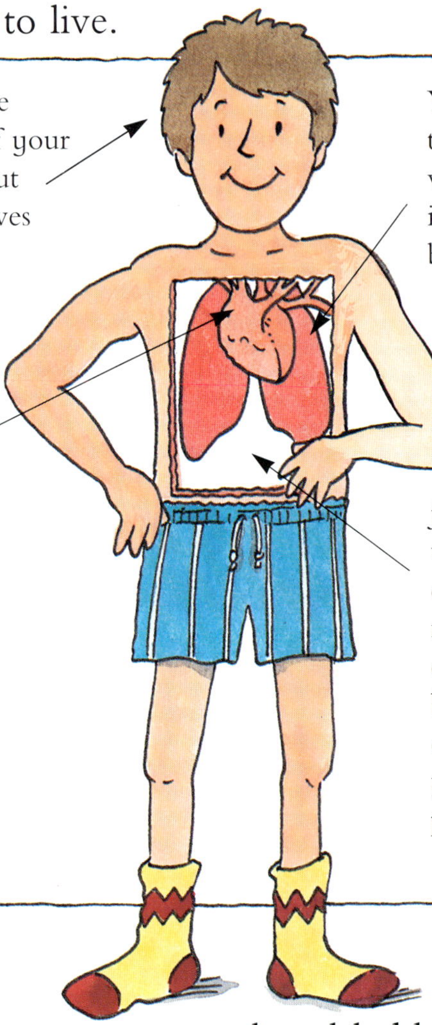

Your brain is the control center of your body. It sends out orders and receives messages.

Your heart is a muscle that pumps blood out to all parts of your body.

Your lungs bring oxygen to your body. They fill with air as you breathe in and empty as you breathe out.

When you eat a meal, food travels down your throat to your stomach. Special juices in the stomach mix with the food to break it down into a watery mixture. Then the parts of the liquid food your body needs are taken away and distributed by your blood. The waste is pushed out of your body.

Bones

Your body parts are protected and held together by a frame of bones called a skeleton. The main part of your skeleton is the spine (or backbone). The ribs protect your heart and lungs. The skull protects your brain.

Your bones have muscles attached to them. If you want to lift your arm, your brain sends a signal to your arm muscle to pull the bone in your arm up.

Strange but True

★ The world's tallest man was 8 feet 11.1 inches high and weighed 439 pounds. The tallest living woman is 7 feet 7.25 inches and weighs 462 pounds.

★ Just by taking a single stride, you use over a hundred different muscles.

Why your body needs sleep

Sleep is a time when your body is resting and making up the energy used during the day. You do most of your growing when you are asleep.

Why your body needs exercise

Everything we do uses muscles. Even when we are resting, many muscles are still at work. Muscles allow your heart to beat, your lungs to take in air, and your stomach to digest food. Muscles become weak and flabby if they are not used enough.

Skin and hair

Skin protects your body against injury and germs. It also helps to keep your body at the same temperature. Hairs grow through the skin on nearly every part of the body, but they are most noticeable on your head.

Nerves

Nerves provide a network of communication throughout your body. When you see something, messages travel along nerves to the brain. Your brain tells you what you have seen. Your senses of hearing, smell, taste, and touch work in the same way. Other nerves control muscles so that you can sit, stand, and walk.

Food

Everyone needs food to stay alive. It gives us the energy to move about and allows our bodies to grow.

A healthy person needs the right amount of the right kinds of food. Millions of people do not have enough to eat. More food is produced each year, and many countries share their food with those who have too little.

Where does food come from?

Some of our food comes from animals. Farmers raise cattle, sheep, pigs, and chickens for their meat. Fishermen go out to sea in boats and catch fish in nets. Fish farmers breed fish in lakes.

Farmers grow crops such as wheat, corn, fruit, and vegetables. Some people grow food plants in their own gardens.

Shopping for food

Much of our food is prepared in factories. It is canned, bottled, frozen or dried to keep it fresh until we eat it.

In a supermarket you can buy all kinds of food from all around the world.

WHY YOUR BODY NEEDS FOOD

You need food to give you energy.

These foods contain sugar and starch, called carbohydrates, which give you energy.

These foods contain proteins. Proteins help you grow and keep you fit and strong.

These foods contain fats. Fats keep you warm, but too much fat is not good for you.

Healthy people eat a mixture of all three kinds of food.

STRANGE BUT TRUE

★ The first people to realize that vitamins were important to health were sailors. On long voyages, they got a disease called scurvy if they could not eat fresh fruit and vegetables. English sailors were given limes to eat, which contain vitamin C. This is why they were called "limeys."

AROUND THE WORLD

Not all crops can be grown in all parts of the world. Some grow best where it is dry and hot. Others prefer plenty of water. People used to eat only the food that grew in their own country. Now food is sold by one country to another.

RICE

Rice is the main food of half of the world's population. It is widely grown in India, Japan, and China. Rice plants like plenty of water. They grow best on flooded land, called rice paddies.

WHEAT

Wheat grows best in dry, mild climates. Most wheat comes from the United States, Northwest Asia, Australia, and China. Mills grind the grain into flour for bread, cakes, and pasta.

POTATOES

The potato plant came from South America, and is now found in many parts of the world. Potatoes can be eaten baked in their skins, or as French fries and potato chips. Sweet potatoes are orange in color and taste quite sweet.

67

Clothes

Most people in the world wear some sort of clothing. What they wear depends on things like the climate and their culture. Because clothes decorate us as well as protect us, styles of clothing change from year to year. This is called fashion.

Clothes through the ages

Early humans wore the skins of animals they had killed to protect themselves against the weather. Later, people learned how to spin thread and weave cloth.

In Greek and Roman times, from 1000 B.C. to A.D. 450, people wore loose, draped tunics.

In the 12th and 13th centuries rich people dressed in velvet and fine silks from the East.

In the 18th century, for the rich, clothes became very grand. Men dressed in silk coats, vests, and knee breeches. Ladies had hoops under their wide skirts. Both men and women wore huge powdered wigs.

In the early 20th century, people dressed in very formal clothes. Out of doors, men wore frock coats and top hats. Ladies carried parasols.

Today we often dress in what is most comfortable.

In the 19th century, a man called Charles Mackintosh invented a waterproof coat. The mackintosh gave off a terrible smell. Since then, people have found much better ways of making rainwear.

TRADITIONAL COSTUME

Many countries have their own traditional costumes. These are often made from materials that are found locally. Today, traditional clothes are usually for special occasions.

Inuit wear thick, warm, long-sleeved jackets made from caribou skin. Their feet are kept warm in sealskin boots.

Arab people wear long, loose robes to keep off the sun. The headdress protects their faces from sandstorms in the desert.

The Japanese kimono is made of silk.

Bolivian clothes are made from llama and alpaca wool. A brightly-colored woollen poncho is worn on top in cold weather.

The Zulu in full battle dress was a fearsome warrior. He wore arm and leg bands made from fur and feathers.

The traditional costume of the New Zealand Maoris is made from flax.

SPECIAL CLOTHING

The clothes people wear often tell us what they do. You can recognize a doctor or a scuba diver immediately from their uniform or equipment. Some people wear protective clothing for their job or for a sport. Divers wear wetsuits to keep them warm in cold waters.

STRANGE BUT TRUE

★ In 12th-century England it was fashionable for men's shoes to have long points. The length of the points showed how important the man was. Noblemen could wear points 2 feet long. Ordinary men were only allowed 6 inches.

69

Sports

There have been sports competitions since the times of ancient Greece and Rome. Running, jumping, and wrestling matches have been organized by most societies since then. Many of the most popular sports were first played in the 19th century.

Olympic games

The earliest recorded Olympic games took place in 776 B.C. Wrestling was the most popular sport. Victors were given a wreath of olive leaves. The modern Olympic games began in Athens in 1896. Now athletes from more than 150 countries compete every two years in the summer or winter Olympics.

Each ring is a different color and represents a continent

Field and track

Gymnasts took part in the ancient Olympic games. Both gymnastics and athletics are important events in the modern Olympic games. Races of up to 400 meters (437 yards) are called sprints. To get a fast start, the athlete places one foot against the starting block. Runners use shoes with spikes that grip the surface of the track. The marathon is the longest race. Runners compete over a 26-mile course.

Winter sports

Skating on ice began in Scandinavia, probably in the 2nd century. Ice hockey was first played in Canada in 1885. Not all skating is on ice: roller skates and skateboards can be used almost anywhere. Ski jumping is a spectacular sport. The skier flies more than 480 feet through the air before landing.

BAT, BALL, AND RACKET

* College football started with a match between Harvard and McGill Universities in 1874. The annual contest to decide the best professional football team is called the Super Bowl.

* The most popular game in the world is soccer, also called Association Football. Competing countries play against each other every four years for the World Cup.

* Baseball is played with nine-player teams. The batter tries to hit a thrown ball and run around four bases before the other team can tag him "out."

* In cricket the batsman hits a ball that is rolled or bounced along the ground. Then he scores points by running back and forth between two wickets.

* In tennis, better rackets have made it a very fast game. Champion players can serve the ball at 130 miles an hour.

Strange But True

* Early versions of soccer and golf were played in China in the 3rd or 4th centuries B.C.

* The marathon celebrates Pheidippides, the messenger who ran from Marathon to Athens to bring news of the Greek victory over the Persians in 490 B.C.

* The Olmecs in 10th-century Mexico played "pok-ta-pok," an early version of basketball that used a fixed stone ring and a solid rubber ball.

IN THE WATER

People of any age can learn to swim and dive. Many people sail, canoe or row in their spare time. Big waves give surfers a thrilling ride.

HOMES

Our homes are built using a wide variety of materials. In cities people often live in apartment blocks built of steel and concrete.

In the past, houses were often built of materials found nearby. Each country has its own style of houses.

THE FIRST HOMES

The earliest people lived in caves. Later, they made huts of mud, grass or reeds. Then they learned how to make round houses from blocks of earth or animal skins. As time went by people made better houses of stone.

HOW PEOPLE USED TO LIVE

By Greek and Roman times, houses were quite large. Wealthy Romans built splendid villas with running water and baths. In the Middle Ages, houses were built of wood and had just one or two rooms. Everyone, including the animals, crowded into them to live, sleep, and eat. Rich people's homes were more elaborate. They were usually built of stone and had many rooms, each for a different purpose.

HOW WE LIVE NOW

Modern houses and apartments are very comfortable. They have different rooms for people to sleep, eat, and relax in. Heating systems and insulating materials keep homes warm and cozy. Large windows make them light and airy.

HOMES THAT MOVE

The Plains Indians lived in skin tents, called tepees. They were easy to take down and could be carried whenever the tribe moved on. The Bedouin people of North Africa still move their homes around in this way.

FLOATING HOMES

In Hong Kong harbor, thousands of people live on houseboats. They use them as fishing boats in the daytime but they eat and sleep on them as well.

STRANGE BUT TRUE

★ Many homes today have some form of central heating. The Romans used under-floor heating in their villas 2,000 years ago.

In the past, the Inuit used blocks of pressed snow to build igloos.

AROUND THE WORLD

In North Africa, many houses have thick mud brick walls and small windows with wooden shutters. The shutters keep out the sun in the daytime and in the evening are opened so that air can flow through and cool the house.

In the mountains of Switzerland, houses have steeply-pitched roofs so that snow can slide off. The houses are built of wood, which is a good insulator and keeps out the cold.

In Borneo, some houses are built above water on stilts. This makes them safe from snakes and wild animals.

73

Occupations

In some parts of the world people work to produce their own food and provide shelter for their families. In industrial countries most people work to earn money. Some occupations are suitable for people who like to work with their hands. Others require many years of study.

Producing food

Many different occupations are involved in producing food. Farmers grow crops and raise cattle for meat. Fishermen catch fish. Millers grind grain into flour, which bakers turn into bread. Other food is processed and packaged by people working in factories. Truck drivers deliver food to the supermarket.

Manufactured goods

In industrial countries, many people are employed in factories that manufacture goods. Designers draw up the plans of what is to be made. Machine operators work on raw materials to produce the finished article. Sales people sell the goods. Managers supervise the workers.

Providing a service

The police, firefighters, and ambulance drivers make our lives safer. Transport workers, waiters, and hotel staff make life more comfortable and convenient. They all provide a service.

Teachers show us how to read and write. They also train people to do all kinds of occupations.

ENTERTAINERS

Some people entertain others as an occupation. Actors, singers, dancers, and musicians perform in front of people. Other entertainers make films, write books or paint pictures for people to enjoy.

HEALTHCARE

When we feel ill, we go to see a doctor. The dentist looks after our teeth. The optician checks our eyes. In the hospital an operation is performed by a surgeon. Patients are cared for by nurses. All these occupations are part of the medical profession.

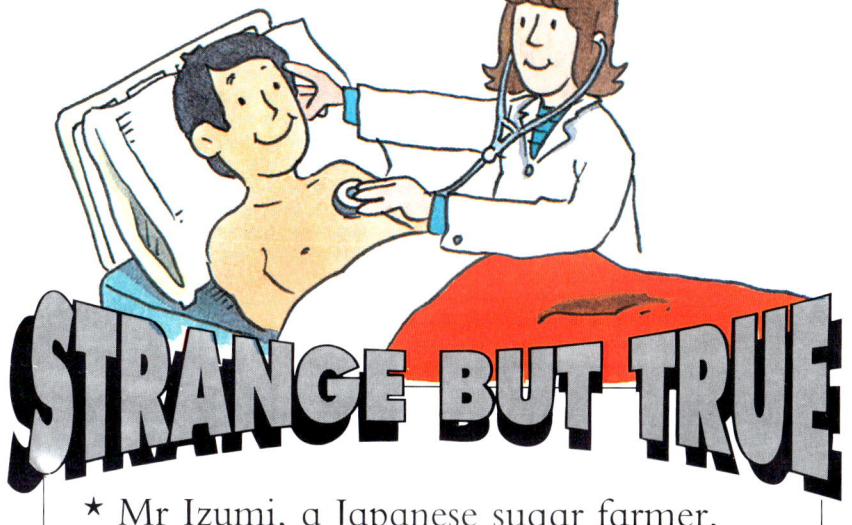

OFFICE WORK

Office workers usually sit at desks for most of the day. They use computers to keep records, work out problems, and send and receive information.

STRANGE BUT TRUE

★ Mr Izumi, a Japanese sugar farmer, worked in the fields for a record 98 years. He retired in 1970, aged 105 and lived to be 120, another record.

★ Some people choose really dangerous occupations. A stunt person takes the place of a film actor when a scene involves a dangerous act like jumping off a building.

Transport

For most of history, riding a galloping horse was the fastest way to travel on land.

Sailboats made great ocean voyages. Then the invention of the steam engine changed land and sea travel forever. Today's transport depends on the gas and the jet engine.

Going by sea

The ancient Egyptians and Chinese had sailboats. Greeks and Romans used boats with oars for war and trade. Explorers voyaging in sailboats discovered and mapped the world. Until the 20th century, vessels sailing the oceans carried cargo around the world. Then came steamships. Today's supertankers and container ships are powered by oil.

The railways

The French TGV and the Japanese Bullet trains carry passengers at high speed between cities as quickly as an airplane. In cities, passengers move around quickly above and under ground in computer-controlled trains. The Bay Area Rapid Transit in California was one of the first systems in the U.S. The first trains were steam powered and the passengers sat in open cars.

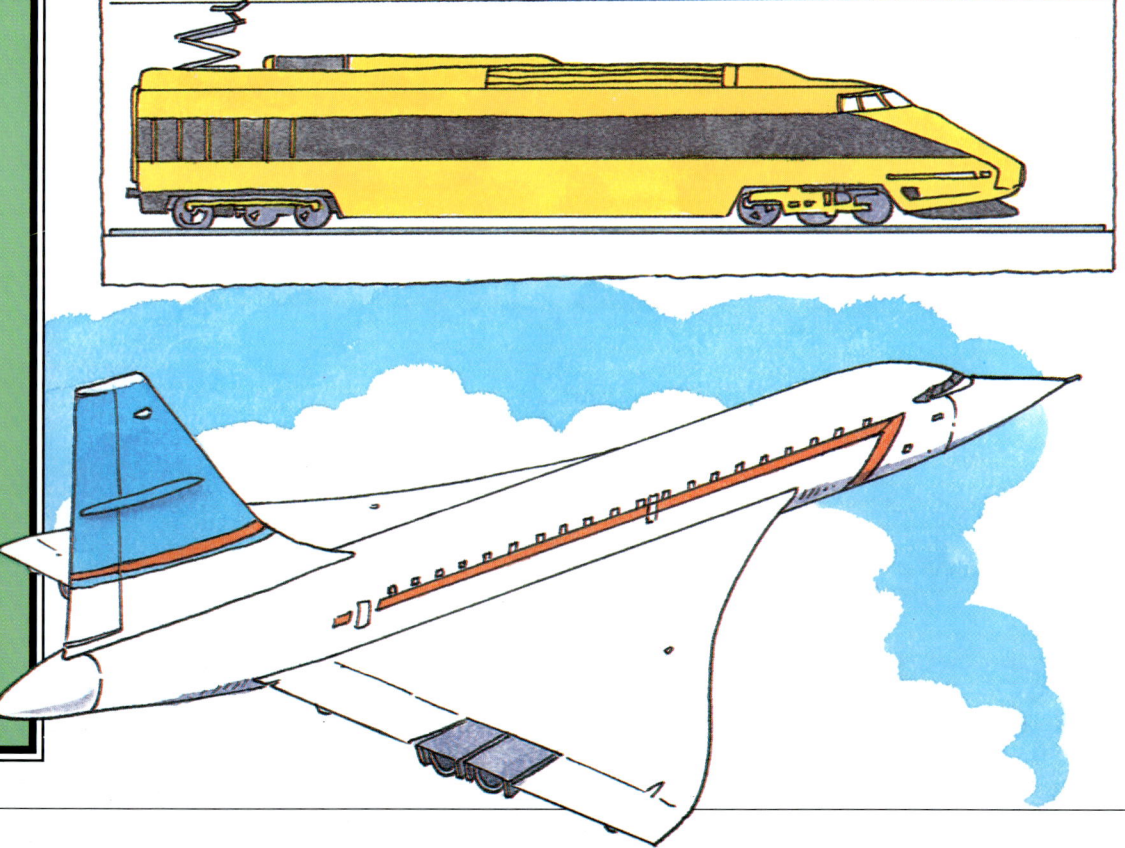

Going by road

The first automobiles were powered by steam engines. In Germany, Karl Benz built the first modern automobile in 1885. It had three wheels, a petrol engine, and a top speed of 9 miles per hour. Today, the automobile is the most popular form of transport.

The Ford Motor Company was first to build 1,000,000 vehicles a year.

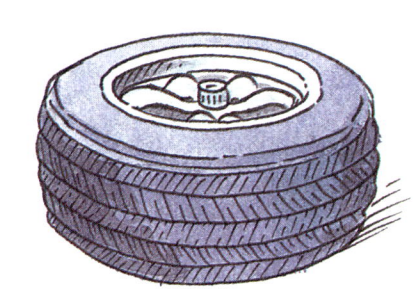

The pneumatic (air-filled) tire was invented by Scotsman John Dunlop in 1888, at almost the same time as the first automobiles. Another Scotsman, John McAdam, invented macadam. This mixture of crushed stones, sand, and tar made the first modern roads.

Flying

Two Americans, Orville and Wilbur Wright, built the first successful airplane. The brothers named their biplane *The Flyer*. Its small gas engine turned propellors. In 1903, Orville made the first flight, 40 yards in 12 seconds. Now Boeing 747s, with four jet engines, regularly fly halfway round the world with 400 passengers.

STRANGE BUT TRUE

★ The first air passengers were a sheep, a duck, and a hen. Their 1783 flight in a hot-air balloon, built by the French Montgolfier brothers, was witnessed by Benjamin Franklin.

★ The average speed of traffic today in many cities is the same as horse-drawn traffic at the beginning of the 20th century.

SPACE

> An ancient Greek, Aristarchos of Samos, worked out that the Earth was round, and that it traveled round the Sun. But not many people listened.

Once people thought the Earth was flat and at the centre of the Universe. Now we know it is part of the Solar System. The Earth is one of the nine planets that go around the Sun. Astronomers used telescopes to discover all the other planets.

THE SOLAR SYSTEM

There are four inner planets. Mercury is closest to the Sun, then Venus, Earth, and Mars. The outer planets are Jupiter, Saturn, Uranus, Neptune, and Pluto, which is farthest from the Sun.

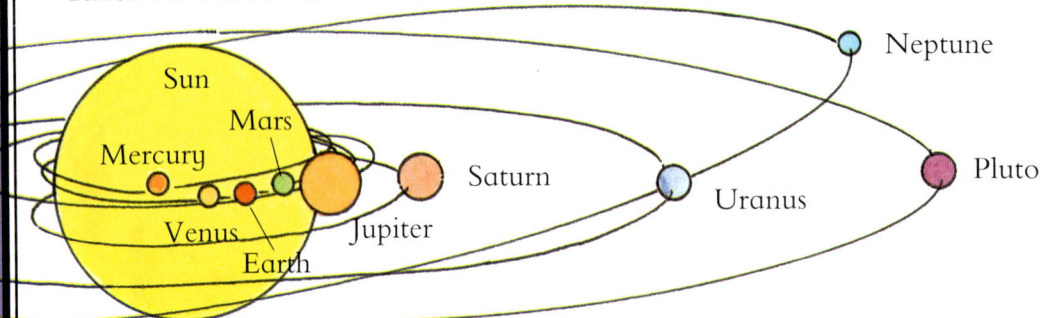

The path, or orbit, that a planet follows is like a slightly flattened circle. This is called an ellipse.

THE UNIVERSE

Our Solar System is part of a galaxy called the Milky Way. Astronomers using powerful telescopes now know that there are many other galaxies in the Universe. Some of the most distant stars have been found because they emit powerful radio signals.

SATELLITES AND PROBES

The first artificial satellite, Sputnik 1, was launched in 1957. Since then, space probes such as Voyager 1 and 2 have flown past the outer planets. Orbiting satellites provide accurate navigation systems for planes and ships, and information for weather forecasters.

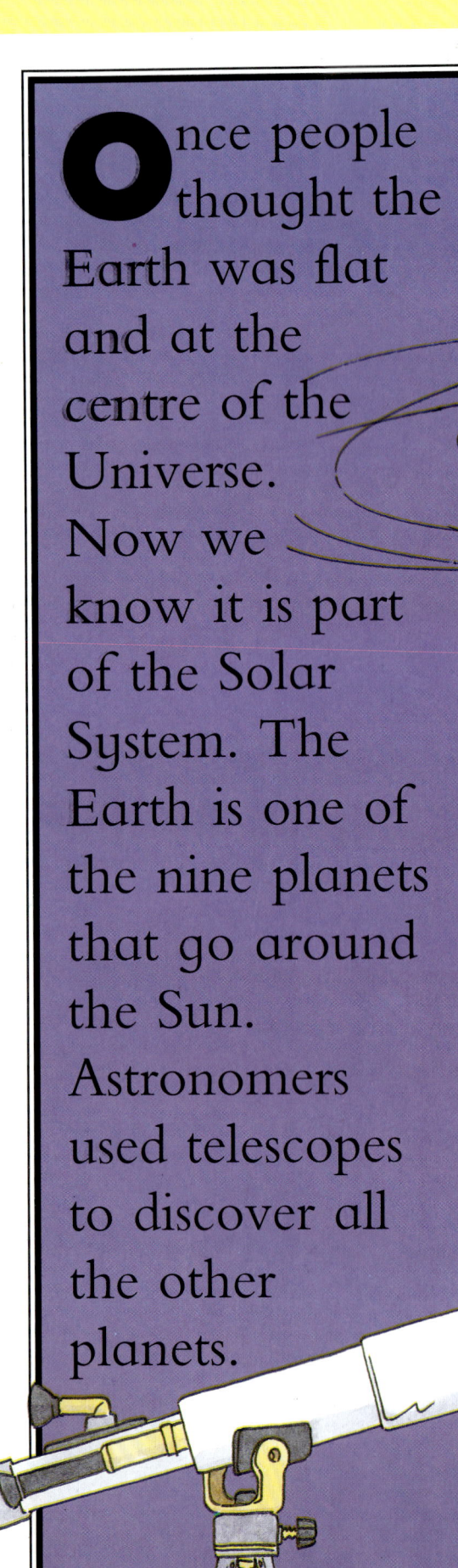

THE MOON AND MARS

In July 1969, American Neil Armstrong became the first person to walk on the Moon. The 11th Apollo mission, powered by a giant Saturn space rocket, took three days to reach the Moon. In 1976, two U.S. robot spacecraft called Viking 1 and 2 landed on Mars. They photographed and examined the surface of the planet and looked for signs of life.

Viking 1

THE SPACE SHUTTLE

The space shuttle is the first space vehicle that can return to Earth and be used again. Including booster rockets and fuel, it weighs more than 2,000 tons, and can carry 39 tons of cargo, and a crew of seven people. The space shuttle is used to put satellites in orbit and for scientific experiments. It has flown successful missions to repair damaged satellites.

STRANGE BUT TRUE

★ The Moon is about 238,857 miles from Earth. It would take you more than 9 years to walk there.

★ A star is formed in our galaxy every 18 days. That means there are 20 new stars each year.

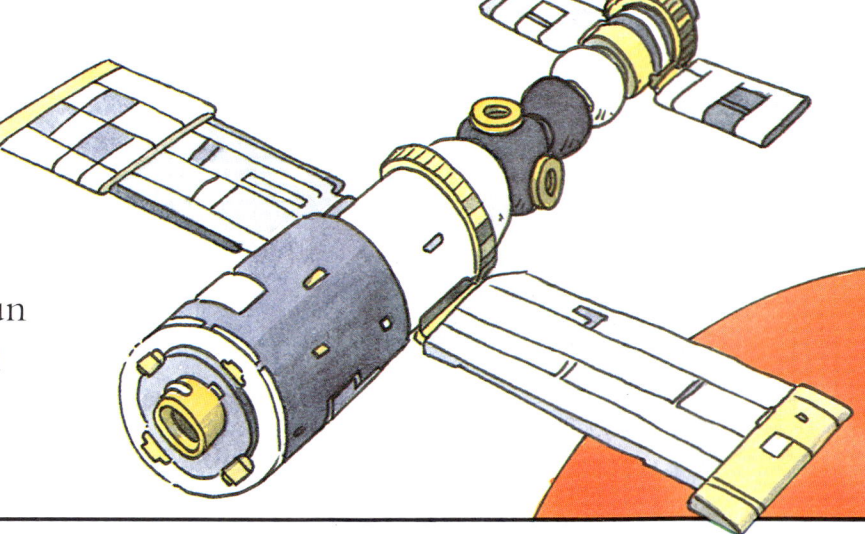

SPACE STATIONS

A space station orbits Earth like a satellite. Astronauts and scientists live and work in it. A space station gets power from solar panels that turn sunlight into electricity. Three crews manned the American space station Skylab before its mission ended in 1974. Two cosmonauts lived on the Russian space station Mir for 366 days.

INDEX

A
air 50
aircraft 42, 43, 48, 76, 77
algae 51
alligator 52
ammonites 54, 55
amphibians 52, 54
Amundsen, Roald 59
animals 44, 45, 47, 51, 52, 53, 54, 55
Arctic Ocean 46, 59
Armstrong, Neil 79
Atlantic Ocean 46, 62
atmosphere 44, 48
Australopithecus 55
Automobiles 77
Aztecs 57

B
Baird, John Logie 63
balls 71
Bardeen, John 63
Bats 71
Bell, Alexander Graham 62
Benz, Karl 77
birds 53
blood 64
boats 58, 76
bones 64
books 42, 60
brain 64, 65
Brattain, Walter 63
butterfly 53

C
camel 45
carbon dioxide 50
carnivore 53
CD player 63
cells 64
chariots 60
Chinese, ancient 56, 60, 76
climate 49
clothing 68, 69
coal 54
Columbus, Christopher 59
compass 58
computers 42, 62, 63, 75
Cook, Captain 59
coral 47
cotton 61
crops 66, 67, 74

D
da Gama, Vasco 59
Dead Sea 47
deserts 45
dinosaurs 55
Diplodocus 55
Drake, Francis 59
Dunlop, John 77

E
Earth, the 44, 45, 46
earthquakes 44
echidna 53
Edison, Thomas Alva 61
Egyptians, Ancient 56, 76
electricity 42, 60, 61
Equator 43, 45, 49
Eriksson, Lief 58
Eskimo 47, 69
Everest, Mount 43
exercise 65
explorers 58, 59

F
factories 66, 74
Faraday, Michael 61
farming 56, 74
fax machine 62
fern 51
field and track sports 70
fish 46, 52, 54, 74
food 53, 64, 65, 66, 67, 74
fossils 54
frog 52
fungus 51

G
Greeks, Ancient 56, 68, 70, 71, 72, 76, 78
gunpowder 56, 58
Gutenberg, Johannes 60

H
hair 65
healthcare 75
heart 64, 65
herbivore 53
hieroglyphics 57
horse 55, 76, 77
hurricanes 48, 49

I
ice 45, 54
Incas 57
Indian Ocean 46, 59, 62
Industrial Revolution 61
insects 53
inventions 42, 60, 61, 62, 63

J
jet engine 76

L
laser 63
lizard 52
lungs 64, 65

M
McAdam, John 77
Macintosh, Charles 69
Magellan, Ferdinand, 59
Maiman, Theodore 63
mammals 52; 53, 55
Marconi, Gugliemo 62
Mars 79
microchip 42, 63
mining 45
Moon 46, 63, 79
Morse, Samuel 62
moss 51
mountains 45
muscles 64, 65

N
Nerves 65
Norsemen 58

O
ocean 46, 47
office work 75
oil 45
Olympic games 70
oxygen 50, 51, 64

P
pachycephalosaur 55
Pacific Ocean 43, 46, 59, 62
Peary, Robert Edwin 59
phonograph 61
photosynthesis 50
planets 43, 44, 78, 79
plants 50, 51, 54
platypus 53
polar bear 45
Poles, North and South 42, 45, 59
Polo, Marco 58
potatoes 67
printing 42, 60
Pterosaurs 55
Pyramids, the 56, 57

Q
Quipu 57

R
radio 42, 62
railways 61, 62, 76
rainforest 43, 51
reptiles 52, 54, 55
rice 67
rivers 45, 48
roads 77
rock 44, 45, 54
Romans, ancient 57, 68, 70, 72, 76

S
satellite 49, 62, 63, 78, 79
Schockley, William 63
Scott, Robert 59
senses 65
services 74
sextant 58
skeleton 64
skin 65
sleep 65
snow 49
Solar System 43, 78
space exploration 45, 62, 79
Space Shuttle 79
steam engine 61, 76
Stegosaurus 55
stomach 64
storms 49
Sun 44, 46, 48, 49, 50, 78

T
telephone 62
television 42, 63
tennis 71
tides 46
trade 58, 59, 76
transformer 61
transistor 63
trees 51
Trevithick, Richard 61
Triceratops 55
trilobites 54
tuatara 53
tyre 77

U
Universe, the 78

V
Venus' flytrap 51
Vikings, the 58
vitamins 67
volcanoes 44

W
water cycle 48
Watt, James 61
weather 48, 49
whale 43, 47
wheat 67
wheels 60
Whitney, Eli 61
winter sports 70
winds 48
world 42, 43, 46
Wright, Orville & Wilbur 77
writing 57

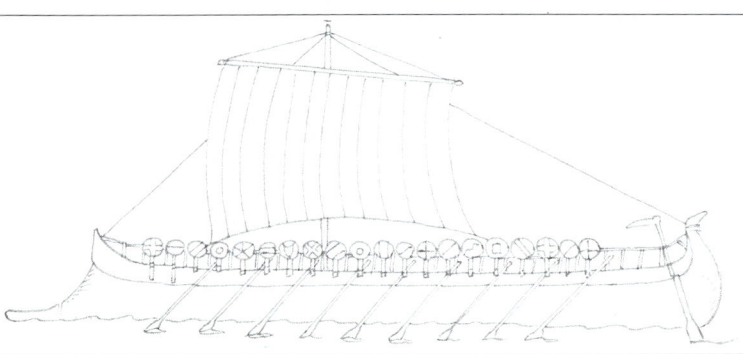

80

PART 3

YOUNG LEARNER'S DICTIONARY

OVER 500 WORDS AND THEIR MEANINGS

Aa Bb Cc Dd Ee Ff Gg Hh Ii Jj Kk Ll Mm

A dictionary is a book of words that are listed in alphabetical order. It tells you what words mean and helps you check how to spell them.

This book explains more than 500 words. Each word, called a **headword**, is printed in heavy black type so that it is easy to find. The headword is followed by a **definition**, printed in ordinary type, which explains the meaning of the word. Some words are illustrated with pictures, to make the meanings clearer.

headword

definition

tiger

illustration

A **tiger** is a wild animal with black and orange stripes. **Tigers** are big cats

To look up a word—for example **tiger**—first look at the letter it begins with. Look at the letters at the top of these pages to find where **t** comes in the alphabet. You can see that it is near the end.

This tells you that the pages listing words beginning with **t** are near the end of the book. To help you, the letters **Tt** in the alphabet at the top of these pages are colored. To find the word **tiger**, look at its second letter and look at words beginning with **ti**. If you cannot find it quickly, look at the third letter and try again.

Nn Oo Pp Qq Rr Ss Tt Uu Vv Ww Xx Yy Zz

The set of 26 letters across the top of the pages is called the alphabet. These are the signs we use to make the thousands of words in the English language.

The word "alphabet" comes from the first two letters of the ancient Greek alphabet, "alpha" and "beta."

Look at the alphabets on the right. They are a few of the different alphabets used around the world today. Some of these letters look very different from the letters in the English alphabet.

АБГДЕЗ
Greek

بِسْمِ ٱللَّهِ ٱلرَّحْمٰنِ
Arabic

ΕΖΗΘΙΚΛ
Russian

The earliest writing used pictures, not words. Thousands of years ago, people in ancient Egypt drew picture symbols, called hieroglyphs.

Aa Bb Cc Dd Ee Ff Gg Hh Ii Jj Kk Ll Mm

Aa

ache
An **ache** is a kind of pain. David's legs **ache** because he ran so fast.

address
Your **address** is the place where you live. When you send a letter, you must write the **address** on it.

air
Air is all around us. We breathe **air** to stay alive.

aircraft
An **aircraft** is a flying machine such as an aeroplane.

alligator
An **alligator** has a long tail and a big mouth full of sharp teeth. **Alligators** live in rivers and swamps.

alphabet
The **alphabet** is the letters people use to write words.

angry
An **angry** person feels very cross and unhappy.

animal
An **animal** is a living thing that is not a plant. People, dogs, birds, frogs, spiders, and fish are all **animals**.

answer
An **answer** is what people want when they ask a question. Jennifer **answered** her dad when he asked her a question.

ant
An **ant** is a tiny insect.

apple
An **apple** is a round fruit that grows on trees.

arm
Your **arm** is the part of your body that is between your shoulder and your hand.

ask
You **ask** a question when you want to know something. You also **ask** when you want to have something.

asleep
When you are **asleep** your body is resting. Eric was so tired, he fell **asleep**.

aunt
Your **aunt** is your father's or your mother's sister. Your uncle's wife is your **aunt**, too.

awake
When you are **awake** you are not asleep. Sarah was still **awake** at ten o'clock.

84

Nn Oo Pp Qq Rr Ss Tt Uu Vv Ww Xx Yy Zz

Bb

baby
A **baby** is a very young child.

back
1. Your **back** is the part of your body behind you from your shoulders to your waist.
2. Mary sat at the **back** of the class.

bad
1. A **bad** person does things that are wrong.
2. A **bad** cold can make you feel ill.

bag
You hold or carry things in a **bag**. Emily had some apples in a paper **bag**.

ball
A **ball** is a round toy. It is used in many games.

balloon
A **balloon** is a small rubber bag you blow into to fill it up with air.

banana
A **banana** is a fruit that grows on trees.

bark
1. **Bark** is the rough covering of a tree.
2. A **bark** is the loud sound a dog makes.

bat
1. A **bat** is a small flying animal. It has a furry body and wings made of stretchy skin. 
2. You use a baseball **bat** to hit the ball in a game.

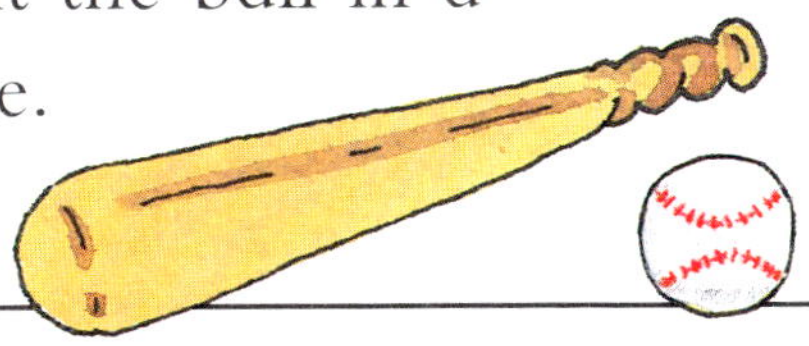

bear
A **bear** is a big furry wild animal. **Bears** can be fierce. 

bed
A **bed** is something you sleep on. It is time to go to **bed**.

bee
A **bee** is a small flying insect.

bend
When you **bend** something you make it crooked.

best
When something is the **best** you like it the most. Jean is Betty's **best** friend.

better
1. Chris plays soccer **better** than he plays baseball.
2. If you are ill, medicine makes you **better**.

85

Aa Bb Cc Dd Ee Ff Gg Hh Ii Jj Kk Ll Mm

bicycle

A **bicycle** is something you ride on. **Bicycles** have two wheels.

big

Big means large. Our car is so **big** you can fit six people inside.

bird

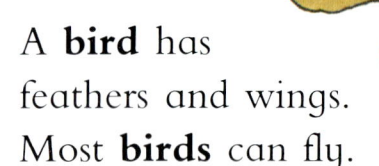

A **bird** has feathers and wings. Most **birds** can fly.

birthday

Your **birthday** is the day of the year you were born. It is Jason's **birthday** on January 16th.

bite

To **bite** something means to cut it with your teeth. Charlene will **bite** into her apple.

blow

To **blow** means to move with air. The wind **blows** the leaves.

boat

A **boat** goes on water. **Boats** are moved by an engine or blown along by the wind.

body

The **body** of a person or animal is every part of them.

bone

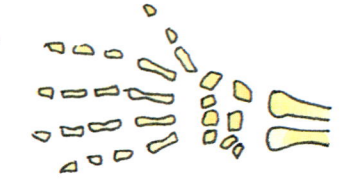

A **bone** is a hard part inside your body. You can feel the **bones** in your fingers.

boot

A **boot** covers your foot and lower leg. Kevin wears rubber **boots** in the rain.

born

When you are **born**, you begin living outside your mother. Nicole's baby sister was **born** last week.

bottle

A **bottle** is something you keep drinks in, such as milk, water or juice.

bottom

1. The **bottom** of something is its lowest part.

2. Your **bottom** is the part of your body on which you sit.

bounce

When a ball **bounces** it hits the ground and then goes up.

box

A **box** is made to hold things. John's toy car came in a red **box**.

86

Nn Oo Pp Qq Rr Ss Tt Uu Vv Ww Xx Yy Zz

bread

Bread is a food made from flour and milk. It is baked in the oven.

break

If something **breaks** it falls to pieces or stops working.

breath

Your **breath** is the air that goes in and out of your body all the time. Alan can hold his **breath**.

breathe

When you **breathe**, air goes in and out of your nose or your mouth.

bring

When you **bring** something you carry it with you. **Bring** a coat, it might get cold.

brother

Your **brother** is a boy who has the same parents you do.

brush

You use a **brush** for cleaning. Tony **brushes** his teeth carefully twice every day.

bud

A **bud** is a shoot that a flower or leaf grows from.

build

When you **build**, you put something together. Katie is **building** a lovely castle from sand.

building

A **building** is a place where people live, work, or play. Houses, hospitals, and schools are **buildings**.

burn

If something **burns,** it is on fire. Tommy's dad **burned** the dinner.

bus

A **bus** is like a big car that carries a lot of people.

busy

When you are **busy** you have things to do. Julie is **busy** writing a letter.

butterfly

A **butterfly** is an insect with four large colored wings.

buy

When you **buy** something you give money for it.

Aa Bb Cc Dd Ee Ff Gg Hh Ii Jj Kk Ll Mm

cake

A **cake** is made of flour, eggs, and sugar. Rebecca had a **cake** on her birthday.

camel

A **camel** is a big animal that lives in hot deserts. **Camels** can live for days without food or water.

camera

You use a **camera** to take photographs or make films.

can

A **can** is a metal container. It often holds food or drink.

car

A **car** is a machine for people to ride in. The roads are busy with **cars.**

card

A **card** is made of stiff paper. **Cards** often have words and pictures on them. Jessica sent me a birthday **card.**

carry

When you **carry** something, you lift it and take it with you. Dad will **carry** a chair into the garden.

cat

A **cat** is a small animal with a long tail. **Cats** have soft fur.

catch

If you **catch** something you grab it or get it while it is moving. Michael threw the ball into the air and Ben tried to **catch** it.

chair

A **chair** is a piece of furniture for one person to sit down on.

change

If you **change** something you make it different. Kevin will **change** his dirty clothes for clean ones.

chase

When you **chase** something you go after it to try to catch it. The man **chased** the letter along the road.

cheese

Cheese is a food made from milk.

chest

1. Your **chest** is the part of your body at the front of you, from your neck to your waist.

2. A **chest** is a heavy box.

child

A **child** is a young boy or girl.

Nn Oo Pp Qq Rr Ss Tt Uu Vv Ww Xx Yy Zz

chin
Your **chin** is part of your face. It is just under your mouth.

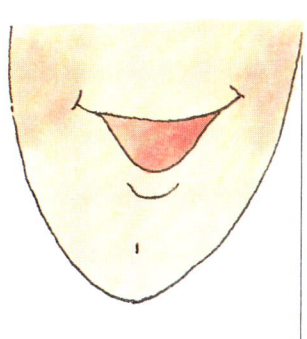

choose
When you **choose** you pick out something you want. Megan **chose** the red shoes.

circle
A **circle** is round like a ring.

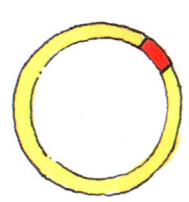

city
A **city** is a busy place full of buildings. Many people live and work in cities.

class
A **class** is a group of people learning things together. The **class** is learning English.

clean
When you **clean** something you take the dirt off it. Joe must **clean** his muddy shoes.

clear
If something is **clear**, you are able to see through it. Windows are made of **clear** glass.

climb
When you **climb** you go up something high. Our cat **climbed** up a tree.

clock
A **clock** shows you the time.

close
1. When you **close** a door, you make it shut.
2. If you are **close** to a person or a thing, you are near them.

clothes
Clothes are the things that people wear to keep themselves warm. Shirts and socks are clothes.

cloud
Clouds float in the sky. They are made of tiny drops of water.

coat
A **coat** is something you put on over your other clothes. When it is cold outdoors, Karen wears her **coat.**

cold
1. A **cold** is something that makes you sneeze and feel ill.
2. If you are **cold** you should put on warmer clothes.

color
1. Red, yellow, pink, green, purple, and blue are different **colors**.
2. When you **color** a picture you put red, blue or some other **colors** on it.

89

Aa Bb Cc Dd Ee Ff Gg Hh Ii Jj Kk Ll Mm

computer
A **computer** is a machine that can remember what you put into it. It can also find answers to questions.

copy
When you **copy** a thing you try to make something just like it. Robert **copied** his sister's drawing.

corner
A **corner** is where two things meet. In a room, the **corner** is where two walls come together.

cough
When you **cough** you make a sudden noise when air is pushed out of your throat. Michael has a bad **cough**.

count
You **count** to find out how many things there are.

country
1. A **country** is an area of land with its own people and language.
2. The **country** is land away from towns with farms and fields.

cousin
The children of your uncle or aunt are your **cousins.**

cover
When you **cover** something you put something over it.

cow
A **cow** is a large animal that lives on a farm. People drink the milk that comes from **cows**.

crash
1. A **crash** is a loud noise.
2. If something **crashes,** it falls or breaks into pieces.

crawl
When you **crawl** you move on your hands and knees.

cry
A **cry** is a noise you make when you are surprised or hurt. A baby **cries** when it needs milk.

cup
A **cup** is something that holds a drink. Joyce poured hot chocolate into a **cup**.

cut
1. When you **cut** something you change its shape with something sharp like scissors.
2. A **cut** is a small place on your skin that you hurt on something sharp.

Nn Oo Pp Qq Rr Ss Tt Uu Vv Ww Xx Yy Zz

Dd

dance
When you **dance** you move your whole body. People **dance** to music.

dangerous
If something is **dangerous** it might hurt you. Some wild animals are **dangerous**.

dark
When it is **dark** there is not enough light to see. If someone has **dark** hair it is usually brown or black.

daughter
If parents have a child who is a girl, she is their **daughter**.

day
1. **Day** is when it is light outside.
2. A **day** is 24 hours.

desert
A **desert** is a hot, dry area of land where very little rain falls.

dessert
Dessert is something sweet that you eat after a meal. Ice cream is a **dessert**.

different
When something is **different** it is not like anything else. That's not Nick's pen. It looks quite **different**.

dig
When people or animals **dig** they make a hole in the ground.

dinosaur
A **dinosaur** is a large animal that lived millions of years ago.

dirty
When something is **dirty** it is not clean. Paul spilled chocolate milk on his T-shirt and made it **dirty**.

disappear
If something **disappears** you cannot see it any more. The magician made the rabbit **disappear**.

dog
A **dog** is a furry animal that barks.

door
A **door** opens to let you into a room.

Aa Bb Cc Dd Ee Ff Gg Hh Ii Jj Kk Ll Mm

draw

When you **draw**, you make a picture of something. Max likes to **draw** cars.

dress
1. You can **dress** yourself when you can put on your clothes without help.
2. A **dress** is a piece of clothing.

drink

When you **drink**, you swallow a liquid such as water. Milk and orange juice are **drinks**.

drop
1. If you **drop** something, you let it fall.
2. A **drop** is a tiny bit of liquid.

dry

If something is **dry**, it has no water in it. Christopher hung up the wet clothes to **dry**.

Ee

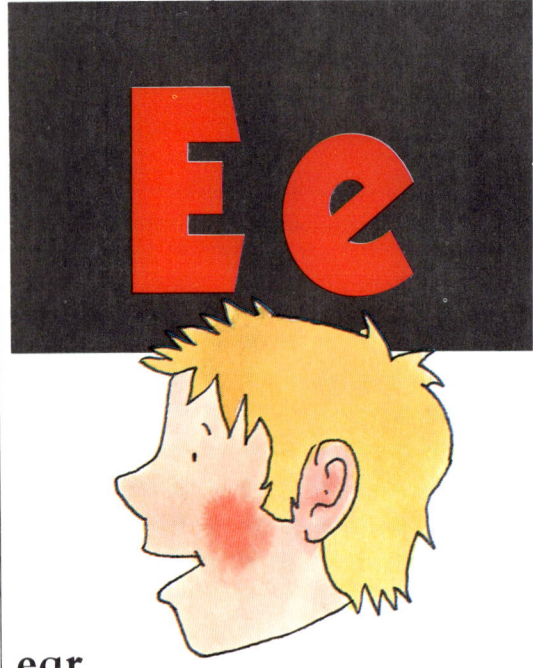

ear

You have two **ears** on your head. You use your **ears** to hear with.

Earth
1. The **Earth** is the world we all live on. 
2. The soil that plants grow in is called **earth.**

easy

If something is **easy**, it is not difficult.

eat

When you **eat**, food goes in your mouth and down your throat to your stomach.

edge

The **edge** is the end or side of something flat. John's toy car fell off the **edge** of the table.

egg

Baby birds, fish, and insects live inside **eggs** until they are ready to be born.

elbow

Your **elbow** is the part of your arm that bends.

elephant

An **elephant** is a very big animal. An **elephant** has a very long nose called a trunk.

empty
1. If something is **empty** there is nothing in it.
2. If you **empty** something, you take out everything in it. Adam **emptied** the bag.

Nn Oo Pp Qq Rr Ss Tt Uu Vv Ww Xx Yy Zz

end
The end of something is the last part. George is standing at the **end** of the queue.

engine
An **engine** is something that makes a machine work. A car **engine** makes the car go.

enjoy
If you enjoy something you like it very much. Sanjay **enjoys** playing with his friends.

evening
Evening is the last part of day, before night. Do you watch television in the **evening**?

exciting
If you think something is **exciting** it is fun and you look forward to it. Traveling by train is **exciting**.

expect
If you **expect** something to happen, you think it will happen. Carla **expects** to win the race.

explain
If you **explain** something to somebody you tell them about it so that they understand.

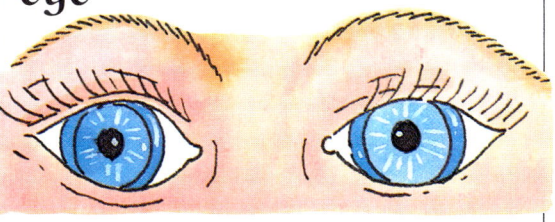

eye
You have two **eyes** at the front of your head. You use your **eyes** to see things. What color are your **eyes**?

Ff

face
Your **face** is the front part of your head. Your eyes, nose, and mouth are on your **face**.

fair
1. If something is **fair**, it is the right thing to do.
2. A **fair** is a place to go and have fun. People buy things at a **fair**.

fall
To **fall** means to drop to the ground. The book **fell** off the table.

farm
A **farm** is a place where people keep animals or grow crops. Uncle Dan has cows on his **farm**.

93

Aa Bb Cc Dd Ee Ff Gg Hh Ii Jj Kk Ll Mm

fast

If someone or something is **fast** they can go very quickly. Nathan is a very **fast** swimmer.

father

A **father** is a man who has children.

favorite

Your **favorite** is the one you like better than all the others. Ice cream is Justin's **favorite** dessert.

feather

Birds have **feathers** to keep them warm instead of fur or hair.

feed

When you **feed** a person or animal you give them something to eat. The mother bird **feeds** her babies.

feel

1. When you **feel** something, you touch it.
2. If you miss lunch you will **feel** very hungry.

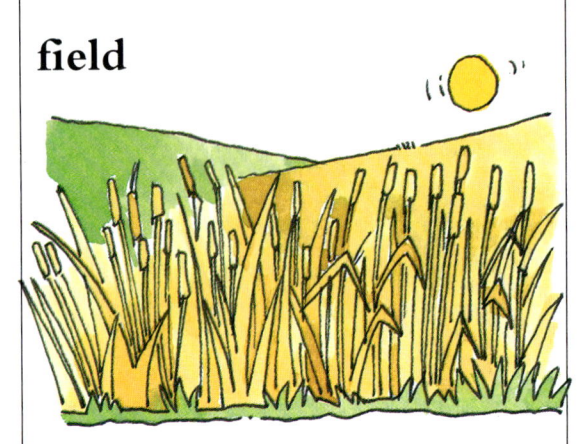

field

A **field** is an open piece of land. Crops are grown in **fields**.

fierce

When an animal is **fierce** it is dangerous. Tigers can be very **fierce.**

fight

A **fight** is when people try to hurt each other. People usually **fight** because they are angry.

fill

If you **fill** something you put in as much as it will hold. Mom **filled** a bag with apples.

film

Film is something you put in a camera to take photographs.

find

When you **find** something you see what you are looking for. Brian **found** his shoes under the bed.

finger

Your **fingers** are part of your hands. People have five **fingers** on each hand.

finish

When you **finish** something you come to the end of it. Jennifer **finished** telling her story.

94

Nn Oo Pp Qq Rr Ss Tt Uu Vv Ww Xx Yy Zz

fire

Fire is what happens when something burns. The **fire** is hot!

first

When something is **first**, nothing else comes in front of it. Neil Armstrong was the **first** person to walk on the moon.

fish

A **fish** is an animal that swims and breathes in water. **Fish** live in seas and rivers.

fit

If something **fits** you it is the right size. Sarah's dress is too big; it does not **fit**.

fix

If somebody **fixes** something they make it work. Ask Dad to **fix** your bike.

flat

1. If something is **flat**, it is straight across.
2. When a balloon is **flat**, it has no air in it.

float

If something **floats**, it stays on top of water and does not go under it. The rubber duck is **floating** in the bath.

floor

The **floor** is the part of a room that you walk on.

flour

Flour comes from a plant called wheat. Bread and cakes are made from **flour**.

flower

A **flower** is part of a plant. **Flowers** often look colorful and smell sweet.

fly

1. To **fly** means to move through the air.
2. A **fly** is an insect with wings.

follow

If you **follow** someone you go along behind them. The children **followed** their mother into the store.

food

Food is what you eat. People and animals need **food** to live.

foot

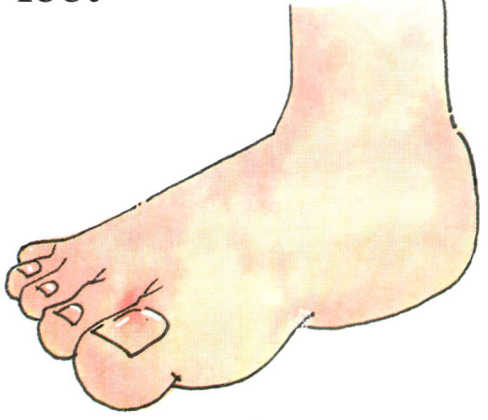

1. Your **foot** is at the end of your leg. You stand on your two **feet**.
2. The **foot** of something is its lowest part. Peter stood at the **foot** of the stairs.

95

Aa Bb Cc Dd Ee Ff Gg Hh Ii Jj Kk Ll Mm

forget
If you **forget** something you do not think of it.

fresh
Fresh means new. Harry enjoys eating **fresh** biscuits.

friend
A **friend** is someone you like being with.

frightened
If you are **frightened** you are afraid. Tommy is **frightened** of spiders.

frog
A **frog** is a small animal that lives near ponds and rivers. **Frogs** have strong back legs that help them to jump a long way.

front
The **front** of something is usually the part that you see first. Alice has a house with a red **front** door.

frozen
Frozen food is kept very cold so that it will remain fresh for a long time.

fruit
Fruit is something to eat. Apples and bananas are different kinds of **fruit**.

full
If something is **full** there is no room left. Sarah's glass was **full** of chocolate milk.

fun
When you have **fun** you enjoy yourself. It is **fun** to play in the snow.

funny
Things that are **funny** make you laugh.

fur
Fur grows on the skin of animals. It keeps them warm.

Gg

game
A **game** is something you play. You can play **games** with your friends.

garage
A **garage** is a building. Cars are kept in **garages**.

garden
A **garden** is a piece of land where you grow flowers and other plants. Zoe likes to play in the back **garden**.

Nn Oo Pp Qq Rr Ss Tt Uu Vv Ww Xx Yy Zz

give
When you **give** something to a person, you let them keep it. Jemma **gave** her friend a birthday present.

glass
1. **Glass** is used to make windows. You can see through **glass**.
2. A **glass** is something you drink from.

good
Something **good** makes you happy. There is a **good** program on TV tonight.

grandfather
Your mother's father and your father's father are both your **grandfathers**.

grandmother
Your mother's mother and your father's mother are both your **grandmothers**.

grass 
Grass is a green plant. Sheep and cows eat **grass**. **Grass** grows in many gardens.

ground
The **ground** is the land you stand on when you are outside.

grow 
When things **grow** they get bigger. The tree had **grown** a lot.

guess
A **guess** is an answer you are not sure is right. **Guess** how old Deborah is?

Hh

hair
Hair grows on people's heads. Dad's **hair** is brown.

hand
People have two **hands**. You use your **hands** to pick things up.

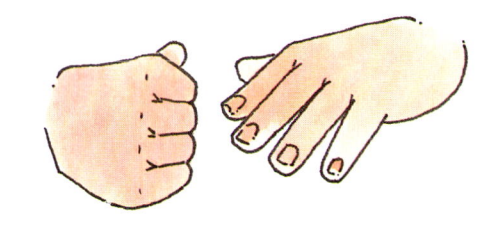

hang
When something **hangs** it is held up from the top. Alex **hung** up his coat.

97

Aa Bb Cc Dd Ee Ff Gg Hh Ii Jj Kk Ll Mm

happen
When things **happen**, they take place. What **happened** in school today?

happy
When you are **happy** you feel good about the way things are.

hard
1. If something is **hard** it does not change shape when you touch it.
2. Something that is **hard** to do can take a long time. Mending the bike was **hard**.

hate
If you **hate** doing something, you do not want to do it. Mark **hates** putting away his toys.

have
1. If you **have** something, you hold it or keep it.

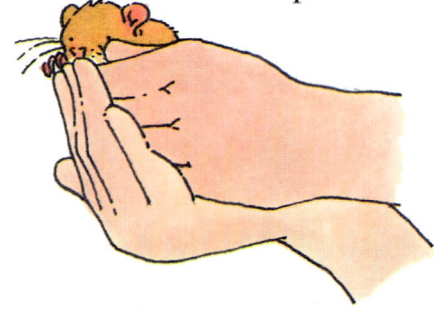

2. You can also **have** a good time at a party.

hear
You **hear** sounds with your ears. I can **hear** a dog barking.

heavy
If something is **heavy** it is hard to lift.

help
When you **help**, you do something for somebody. Do you need **help** carrying the bag?

hide
If you **hide** something you put it where people cannot see it. Katherine **hid** the ball in the cupboard.

high
If something is **high**, it is a long way up. Emily's kite flew very **high** in the air.

hill
A **hill** is a high part of the land.

hit
If you **hit** something, you touch it quickly and hard. Jessica **hit** the ball a long way.

hold
If you **hold** something, you keep it in your hands or arms.

hole
1. A **hole** is a place that has been dug in the ground.
2. A **hole** is also a space in something. The mouse went into a **hole** in the wall.

home
Your **home** is the place where you live.

hope
If you **hope** for something, you want it to happen and think it will. Claire **hopes** to get a kitten soon.

Nn Oo Pp Qq Rr Ss Tt Uu Vv Ww Xx Yy Zz

horse
A **horse** is a big animal that you can ride. In the past, **horses** worked on farms.

hospital
A **hospital** is a place where ill people are made better.

hot
Hot things burn if you touch them.

hour
An **hour** is a measure of time. There are sixty minutes in one **hour**, and twenty-four **hours** in one day.

house
A **house** is a building that people live in.

hungry
When you are **hungry** you want to eat.

hurricane
A **hurricane** is a very strong storm that can blow down trees and buildings.

hurry
When you **hurry** you move quickly.

hurt
When something **hurts**, it is painful. Josh **hurt** his knee when he fell.

husband
A **husband** is a man who is married.

Ii

ice
Ice is frozen water that feels cold and hard.

ice cream
Ice cream is a frozen food made of flavored cream.

idea
When you have an **idea** you think of something to do.

important
Important things matter a lot. It is **important** to look and listen for traffic before you go across a road.

insect
An **insect** is a small animal with six legs. Ants, flies, and bees are **insects**.

99

Aa Bb Cc Dd Ee Ff Gg Hh Ii Jj Kk Ll Mm

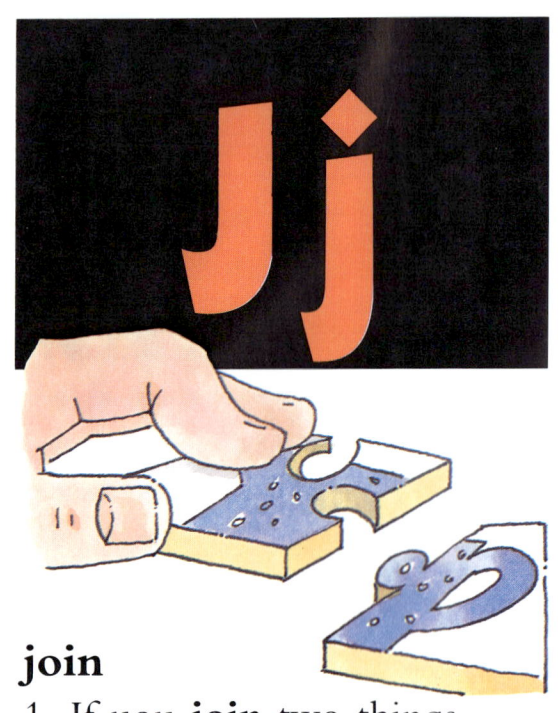

Jj

join
1. If you **join** two things, you put them together.
2. If you **join** a game, you become part of it.

joke
A **joke** is something to make you laugh. Dad put on a toy red nose as a **joke**.

juice
Juice is the drink that comes from fruit like oranges.

jump
When you **jump** you bend your knees and push up into the air. Cassie **jumped** high to catch the ball.

Kk

kangaroo
A **kangaroo** is a big animal with strong back legs. It moves along by jumping.

keep
1. If you **keep** something you have it.
2. To **keep** quiet is to stay quiet.

kick
If you **kick** a ball you hit it with your foot. Dan gave the ball a hard **kick**.

kind
1. **Kind** means a group of things that are like each other. Bananas are a **kind** of fruit.
2. Someone who is **kind** thinks of other people and is good to them.

kiss
When you **kiss** someone you touch them with your lips. Mary gave Grandma a **kiss**.

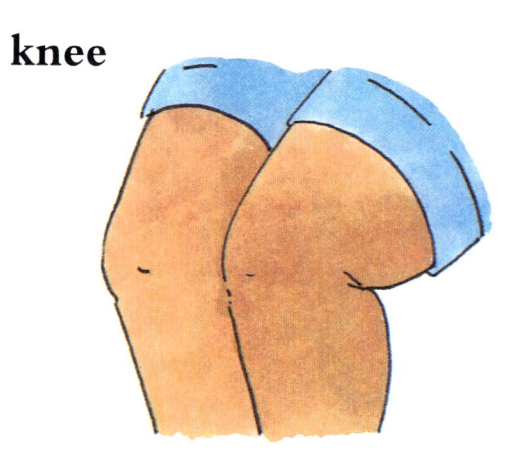

knee
Your **knee** is the place where your leg bends. Ben fell and hurt his **knee**.

know
If you **know** something, you are sure about it.

Nn Oo Pp Qq Rr Ss Tt Uu Vv Ww Xx Yy Zz

Ll

ladder
You use a **ladder** to climb up to and down from high places. Alan must use a **ladder** to get his cat down from the tree.

lamp
A **lamp** gives you light. James has a reading **lamp** by his bed.

land
1. **Land** is the dry part of the Earth.
2. When something **lands** it comes down from the air on to the ground.

last
When something is **last**, there is nothing else after it. Christopher ate the **last** piece of cake.

laugh
A **laugh** is the sound you make when you are happy, or when you think something is funny.

leaf
A **leaf** is part of a plant. Most **leaves** are flat and green.

learn
When you **learn**, you find out something you did not know. Belinda **learned** to write last year.

left
You have a **left** side and a right side. In this picture, the boy is on the **left**.

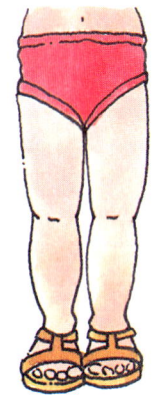

leg
Your **legs** are part of your body. You use your **legs** for standing, walking, and running.

lemon
A **lemon** is a yellow fruit that tastes sour.

lesson
A **lesson** is something you learn. Tony's class had a writing **lesson** in school this morning.

letter
1. **Letters** make up words. A, B, and C are **letters**.
2. A **letter** is a message you write on paper and send to another person.

101

Aa Bb Cc Dd Ee Ff Gg Hh Ii Jj Kk Ll Mm

lift
If you **lift** something, you pick it up. The bag was too heavy for Maggie to **lift**.

light
1. We need **light** to see by.
2. If something is **light** it is easy to lift.
3. If somebody **lights** a fire, they start it burning.

lightning

Lightning is a quick line of light in the sky. **Lightning** happens in a thunderstorm.

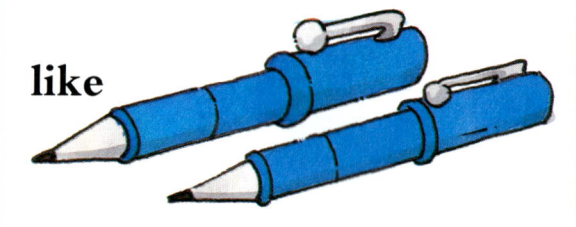

like

1. When one thing is **like** another thing, they are the same.
2. If you **like** a person, you feel happy with them.

line
1. A **line** is long and thin. Hazel drew a straight **line**.
2. A **line** is a row of things.

lion
A **lion** is a wild animal. It is a big cat that lives in the jungle.

lip
Your **lips** are part of your mouth. You have two **lips**.

listen
When you **listen** to something you try and hear it as well as you can.

little
Little things are very small. The baby has **little** shoes.

live
1. To **live** is to be alive. Old people have **lived** for a long time.
2. When you **live** somewhere your home is there.

long
1. When something is **long**, the two ends are far apart.
2. **Long** is a measure of time. Is it a **long** time until your birthday?

look
You **look** at things with your eyes. **Look** at that bird.

loose
If something is **loose**, it is not tight. Molly's front tooth is **loose**.

lose
1. If you **lose** something, you don't know where it is.
2. If you **lose** a race you do not win.

loud
Something **loud** makes a lot of noise. Matt has a very **loud** voice.

love
Love is a very strong feeling for a person. If you **love** someone, you care about them very much.

low
Something **low** is not high up. Beatrice's television is on a **low** table.

Nn Oo Pp Qq Rr Ss Tt Uu Vv Ww Xx Yy Zz

Mm

machine
Machines help people to do things. A **machine** often has parts that move. You wash your clothes in a washing **machine**.

make
1. If you **make** something, you put it together.
2. You can **make** something happen. Richie **made** the baby laugh.

married
A man and woman who are **married** are husband and wife.

measure
If you **measure** something, you find out how big or heavy it is. Dad **measured** how tall Sonya had grown.

meat
Meat is part of an animal that people eat. Hamburgers are made of **meat**.

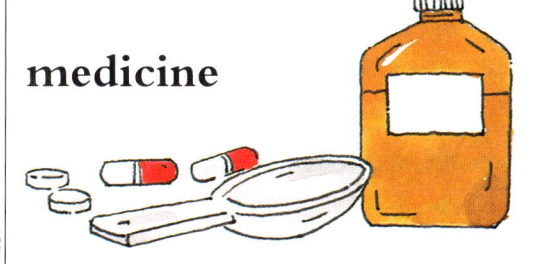

medicine
Medicine is something that helps ill people to get better. When John had a cough his dad gave him **medicine**.

meet
If you **meet** someone, you get together with them. Mum **met** Marsha at school.

metal
Metal comes from the ground. Iron and silver are different kinds of **metal**. **Metal** is for making things like cars and machines.

middle
If you are in the **middle** of a row, you have the same number of people on each side of you.

milk
Milk is a drink. Most of the **milk** that people drink comes from cows.

minute
A **minute** is a measure of time. There are sixty seconds in a **minute**.

miss
1. If you **miss** something you do not get it.
2. If you **miss** somebody, you are sorry they are not there.

mistake
If you make a **mistake** you get something wrong. I made a **mistake** in my spelling.

mix
When you **mix** things you put them together to make one thing.

103

Aa Bb Cc Dd Ee Ff Gg Hh Ii Jj Kk Ll **Mm**

money
You use **money** to buy things. **Money** can be coins or paper.

monkey

A **monkey** is a small animal that climbs trees. **Monkeys** have strong hands and tails.

month
A **month** is a measure of time. There are twelve **months** in a year.

Moon

At night, you can often see the **Moon** in the sky. It goes around the Earth once every 28 days.

morning
Morning is the part of the day up to lunchtime.

mother
A **mother** is a woman who has children.

mountain

A **mountain** is a high piece of land that goes up into a point. **Mountains** are like very big hills.

mouse

A **mouse** is a small, furry animal. It has a pointed nose, sharp teeth, and a long, thin tail.

mouth
Your **mouth** is part of your face. You open and close your **mouth** to speak and to eat.

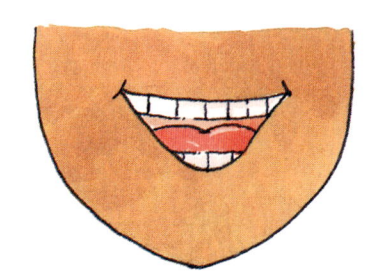

Nn

name
A **name** is what people or things are called. My friend's **name** is Julia.

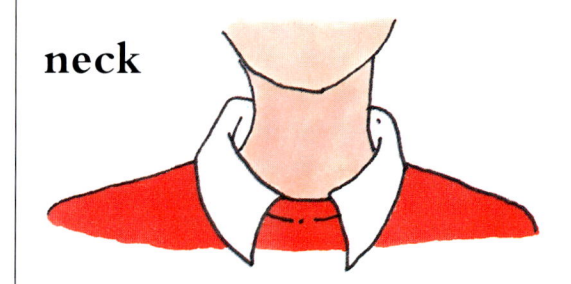

neck

Your **neck** is the part of your body from your head to your shoulders.

need
If you **need** something you must have it. Kay **needs** to have new shoes.

nephew
The son of a person's sister or brother is their **nephew**.

104

Nn Oo Pp Qq Rr Ss Tt Uu Vv Ww Xx Yy Zz

new

New things have not been used. Cindy was given a **new** dress for the party.

niece

The daughter of a person's sister or brother is their **niece**.

night

Night is when the sky is dark.

noise

A **noise** is a kind of sound. The children shouted and made a lot of **noise**.

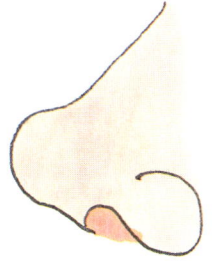

nose

Your **nose** is part of your face. You smell things with your **nose**.

number

You use **numbers** when you count things or people. One hundred is a big **number**.

Oo

old

1. If someone is **old** they have lived for a long time.
2. You say something is **old** if you have used it a lot.

open

If something is **open** it is not covered or shut. Will you **open** the door for me, please?

orange

An **orange** is a round, juicy fruit that grows on trees.

outside

If you are **outside**, you are not in a building. When it is sunny, we like to go **outside** to play.

owl

An **owl** is a bird. **Owls** fly at night.

Pp

pain

A **pain** is what you feel when you are hurt or ill. When Lee fell off his bike he had a bad **pain** in his arm.

paint

When you **paint** something, you put color on it. What color **paint** shall we use for the door?

paper

You can write or draw on **paper**. Colored **paper** can be used to wrap gifts.

105

Aa Bb Cc Dd Ee Ff Gg Hh Ii Jj Kk Ll Mm

park
1. A **park** is a place with grass and trees. People rest or play games in a **park**.
2. If someone **parks** a vehicle, they leave it somewhere for a while. Mom **parked** the automobile in the garage.

part
A **part** of something is a piece of it. Your arm is **part** of your body.

party
A **party** is a group of people having a good time. Tim will have a **party** on his birthday.

pencil
A **pencil** is a wooden stick with black or color inside. You draw or write with a **pencil**.

photograph
A **photograph** is a picture you make with a camera. Dad **photographed** Daniel playing in the sand.

piano
A **piano** is a musical instrument. You play the **piano** with your fingers.

pick
1. When you **pick** things like flowers or fruit, you take them from the place where they grow.
2. If you **pick** things up, you lift them.
3. If there are things to choose from, you **pick** the one you want.

picture
A **picture** is something you draw. Marie drew a **picture** of her sister.

piece
A **piece** of something is a bit of it. Would you like a **piece** of cake?

pig
A **pig** is an animal that lives on a farm. We eat meat from **pigs**.

place
A **place** is where something happens or where something is. Let's find a good **place** for our party.

plain
1. A **plain** is a large, flat part of land.
2. If something is **plain**, it is all one color.

plant
A **plant** is something living that grows in soil. Many **plants** have leaves and colorful flowers.

plate
A **plate** is flat and round. You eat your food from a **plate**.

Nn Oo Pp Qq Rr Ss Tt Uu Vv Ww Xx Yy Zz

play
1. When you **play**, you do something that is fun.
2. If you **play** music, you make music.

playground

A **playground** is a place where children can play. Bill likes to play on the slide in the **playground**.

point
1. The **point** of something is the sharp end of it.
2. You **point** your finger to show the way, or to show where something is.

pour
When you **pour** something, you tip it out. Roger **poured** some milk from the bottle.

present
A **present** is something that people give. Julian had lots of **presents** on his birthday.

promise
If you **promise** something, you are saying you are sure you will do it. Betty **promises** to take the dog for a walk.

pull

When you **pull** something, you move it towards you.

push
When you **push** something, you move it away from you. Catherine **pushed** open the door with her hand.

put
If you **put** something in a place, you make it go there. Tom **put** the food on the plate.

Qq

question
You ask a **question** when you want to know something.

quick
When something is **quick**, it does not take a long time.

quiet
If you are **quiet**, you do not make any noise. The class was very **quiet**.

107

Aa Bb Cc Dd Ee Ff Gg Hh Ii Jj Kk Ll Mm

Rr

rabbit
A **rabbit** is a small, furry animal. **Rabbits** have long ears and short, fluffy tails.

race
When you run a **race**, you find out who goes the fastest. Sam will **race** you to the store.

rain
Rain is water that falls in drops from the sky.

rainbow
A **rainbow** is a band of colors you can sometimes see in the sky. **Rainbows** happen when there is sun and rain together.

read
People who **read** can understand words written down.

ready
When you are **ready**, you can start to do something. Are you **ready** to go to school?

remember
When you **remember** something, you can think of it again. Do you **remember** when we sailed in the boat?

rest
When you **rest**, you stay quiet for a while. Grandma has a **rest** every day.

rhyme
When words **rhyme**, they have the same sound. Cat and bat are words that **rhyme**.

ride
When you **ride** something, you sit on it as it moves along. Would you like a **ride** on my bike?

right
1. You have a left side and a **right** side. Many people write with their **right** hand.
2. If you are **right** about something, you know the answer.

ring
1. A **ring** is something you wear on your finger.
2. A **ring** is also the sound made by the telephone.

river
A **river** is a lot of water flowing across the land.

Nn Oo Pp Qq Rr Ss Tt Uu Vv Ww Xx Yy Zz

road
A **road** is a narrow, clear piece of land. People build **roads** for automobiles to drive on.

rock
Rocks are very hard, big stones in the earth.

roll
1. When something **rolls**, it turns over and over.
2. A **roll** is a small piece of bread.

room
1. A **room** is part of a house or other building.
2. **Room** also means space. Is there enough **room**?

row
If people or things are in a **row**, they are in a line. Natalie put her toy cars in a **row**.

run
When you **run**, you go as fast as you can on foot.

Ss

safe
When you are **safe**, nothing bad can happen to you.

salt
Salt is something that some people put on food to alter its taste.

same
Things that are the **same** are alike. Jasmine's eyes are the **same** color as her sister's.

sand
Sand is tiny pieces of rock. You find **sand** in deserts and on beaches.

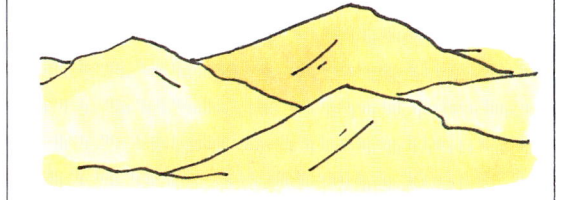

say
When you **say** something, you speak. Jeffrey **says** he is going to the park.

scare
If something **scares** you, it makes you feel frightened.

school
School is a place where people go to learn things.

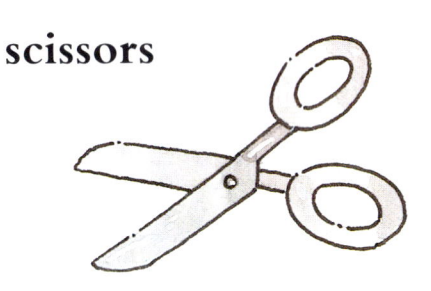

scissors
Scissors have two sharp parts joined in the middle. You use **scissors** for cutting.

sea
The **sea** is a very large area of salty water.

second
1. **Second** is the next thing after first.
2. A **second** is a measure of time.

109

Aa Bb Cc Dd Ee Ff Gg Hh Ii Jj Kk Ll Mm

see
When you **see**, you use your eyes to look at something. Can you **see** those birds?

seed
A **seed** is the part of a plant that will grow into another plant.

send
If you **send** something, you make it go somewhere else. Pat **sent** Grandpa a birthday card.

shape
A **shape** is the way something looks. The letter Z has a zigzag **shape**.

share
If you **share** something, you give a part of it to somebody else. Amanda and her sister **shared** an apple.

sharp
Something **sharp** is easy to cut with. You must be careful with **sharp** scissors.

sheep
A **sheep** is an animal that lives on a farm. **Sheep** are kept for wool and meat.

sheet
1. A **sheet** is a large piece of cloth you put on a bed.
2. A **sheet** of paper is a flat piece of paper.

shell
A **shell** is a hard cover. A snail has a **shell** on its back.

ship
A **ship** is a large boat that carries people and things.

shoe
Shoes are things you wear on your feet. You can walk outside in **shoes**.

shop
A **shop** is another name for a small store. Mom wants to **shop** for a dress.

short
1. A **short** person is not very tall.
2. A **short** walk does not take a long time.

shoulder
Your **shoulder** is the place where your arm joins your neck.

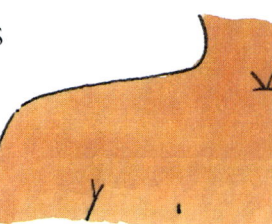

shout
You **shout** when you make a loud noise with your voice.

show
1. You **show** something when you let a person see it.
2. A **show** is something you see. Fiona went to see the magician's **show**.

Nn Oo Pp Qq Rr Ss Tt Uu Vv Ww Xx Yy Zz

shut

If something is **shut**, it is not open. Please **shut** the window.

shy

A **shy** person does not enjoy meeting new people. Josephine was too **shy** to go to the party.

side

1. A **side** is a part of something.
2. In a game, people play on different **sides**.

sing

People who **sing** make music with their voices.

sister

Your **sister** is a girl who has the same parents as you.

sit

To **sit** means to rest on your buttocks. The children **sat** on the floor.

size

Size is how big something is. These shoes are the wrong **size**!

skin

Skin is the thin outer cover of living things. An apple has a thin **skin**.

sky

The **sky** is all the space above you outside. The Sun, Moon, and stars are in the **sky**.

sleep

You **sleep** when you close your eyes and rest your whole body. Terry needs more **sleep**.

slide

1. When you **slide**, you move along easily on something slippery, like ice.
2. A **slide** is something you play on.

slip

If you **slip**, you slide too fast and fall down. Lynn **slipped** on the wet grass.

slow

Slow people or animals don't move very quickly. Snails are very **slow**.

small

Small things are quite little. Most insects are **small**.

smell

If food has a bad **smell**, usually it is not fresh. You **smell** things with your nose.

smile

When you **smile**, the ends of your mouth go up. The baby gave a **smile**.

111

Aa Bb Cc Dd Ee Ff Gg Hh Ii Jj Kk Ll Mm

smoke

Smoke is the dark cloud that comes from something burning.

snail

A **snail** is a very small animal with a shell on its back. **Snails** move by sliding slowly along the ground.

sneeze

When you **sneeze**, air blows out of your nose and mouth with a loud noise. Sam **sneezes** when he has a cold.

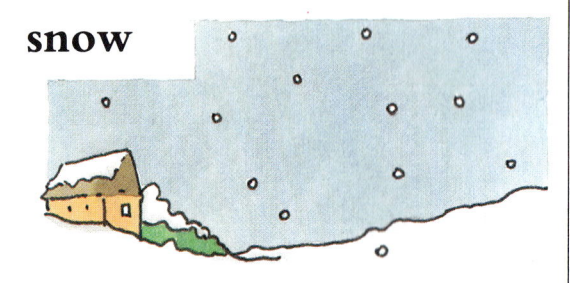

snow

Snow is frozen water that falls from the sky. **Snow** is soft and white.

soap

People clean themselves with **soap**.

sock

Socks are soft clothes you wear on your feet.

soft

1. If you touch something **soft**, it does not feel hard.
2. A **soft** noise is very quiet.

son

If parents have a child who is a boy, he is their **son**.

sorry

You are **sorry** when you feel bad about something. Ronnie is **sorry** he cannot come to the party.

sound

A **sound** is something you can hear. That **sounds** like a dog barking.

sour

Something that is **sour** has a sharp taste. Lemons are **sour**.

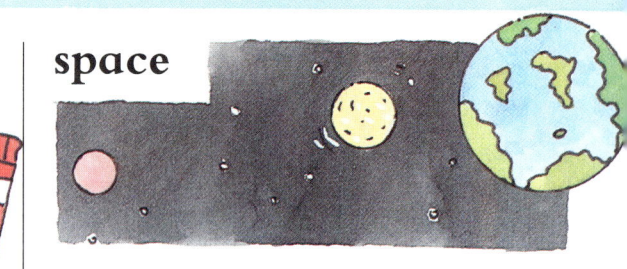

space

1. A **space** is like a hole or a place with nothing in it.
2. The Moon, Sun, and Earth are all in **space**.

speak

When you **speak**, you say words. Please **speak** quietly.

special

Something that is **special** is important and different from anything else. Mum made a **special** dress for the party.

speed

Speed is how fast something goes. What **speed** can your car go?

spell

When you **spell** a word, you put the letters in the right places. C-A-T **spells** cat.

spend

To **spend** money or time means to use it. Would you like to **spend** a day at the zoo?

Nn Oo Pp Qq Rr Ss Tt Uu Vv Ww Xx Yy Zz

spider

A **spider** is a small animal with eight legs. **Spiders** build webs and catch insects to eat.

square

A **square** is a shape that has four sides all the same. The rooms in Martha's house are all **square**.

stairs

Stairs are a set of steps inside a house or other building.

stand

When you **stand**, you are on your feet. We **stood** in a queue to get into the cinema.

star

A **star** is really a sun far away in space. On a clear night, you can see **stars** shining brightly in the sky.

state

A **state** is one part of a country. There are fifty **states** in the U.S.A.

stay

When you **stay** in a place, you don't leave it. Ed has to **stay** in his room to finish his homework.

step

1. You take a **step** when you pick up your foot and move it to a different place.
2. A **step** is also something you walk on to go up or down.

stick

1. A **stick** is a long, thin piece of wood.
2. You can **stick** a poster on the wall with tape.

stone

1. A **stone** is a small rock that comes out of the ground.
2. **Stone** is a strong, hard material that is used to make buildings.

stop

If you **stop** doing something, you don't do it any more. Angie **stopped** reading.

store

To **store** is to keep something. The squirrel **stored** nuts for the winter.

storm

When there is a **storm**, it rains or snows and it is very windy. Thunder and lightning sometimes happen in **storms**.

story

A **story** is about something that has happened. Some **stories** are made up, and some are about real things.

straight

Something that is **straight**, does not bend. Can you draw a **straight** line?

strange

If something is **strange**, it is new to you.

113

Aa Bb Cc Dd Ee Ff Gg Hh Ii Jj Kk Ll Mm

street

A **street** is a road with buildings on it.

stretch

When something **stretches**, it becomes longer. I **stretched** to reach the top shelf.

strong

1. If something is **strong** it does not break easily.
2. **Strong** winds blow very hard.
3. Someone who is **strong** can lift heavy things easily.

sugar

Sugar is sweet and made from plants. People put **sugar** in foods and drinks to make them taste sweet.

sun

The **Sun** is in the sky. It gives us heat and light.

sure

If you are **sure** something is true, you know you are right about it.

surprise

A **surprise** is something you do not know about before it happens. Mom and Dad **surprised** Theresa on her birthday.

sweet

Things that are **sweet** have lots of sugar in them. Cakes and ice cream are **sweet**.

swim

When you **swim,** you move your arms and legs to go along in the water.

table

A **table** has legs and a flat top. Hurry now, the food is on the **table**.

tail

A **tail** grows at the back end of some animals. Dogs and cats have **tails**.

talk

When you **talk** you speak words. Shaun's baby sister is learning to **talk**.

tall

Someone who is **tall** has grown higher than other people. Wayne's dad is **taller** than his mom.

Nn Oo Pp Qq Rr Ss Tt Uu Vv Ww Xx Yy Zz

taste

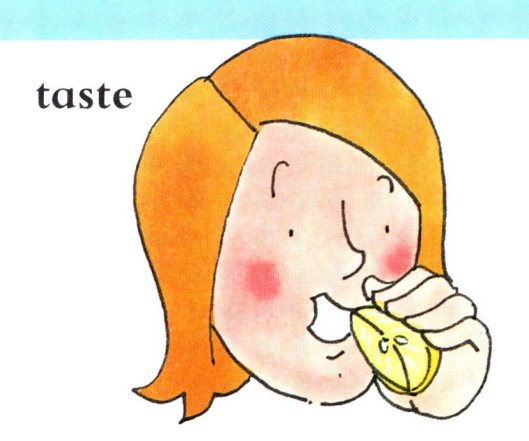

When you **taste** something, you feel it with your mouth and tongue. Lemons **taste** sour.

teach

When somebody **teaches** you, they help you learn how to do something. Mom will **teach** Nicola to swim.

team

A **team** is a lot of people working or playing together. You need two **teams** to play football.

tear

You **tear** something when you pull it apart. James's dog likes to **tear** paper.

teeth

Your **teeth** are inside your mouth. You use your **teeth** for eating food.

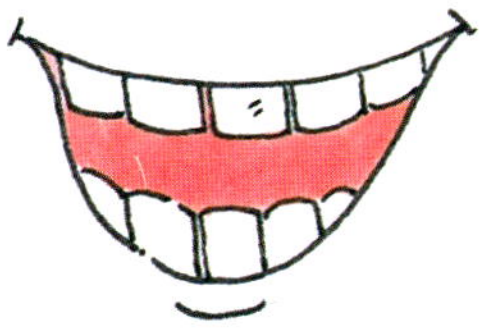

telephone

A **telephone** lets you talk to someone who is somewhere else. A shortened word for **telephone** is **phone**.

television

You can see pictures and hear sounds on a **television**. **TV** is a shortened name for **television**.

tell

If somebody **tells** you something they let you know about it. **Tell** Mom what you did at school.

temperature

The **temperature** of something is how hot or cold it is.

think

When you **think** about something, you have it in your mind. Can you **think** about a present for Mom?

thirsty

If you are **thirsty**, you want something to drink.

throat

Your **throat** is the part of your body that is inside your neck. When you are thirsty, your **throat** feels dry.

throw

When you **throw** something you send it through the air with your hand. Philippa **threw** the ball a long way.

thumb

Your **thumb** is the digit near your wrist. Your **thumb** helps you pick up things.

thunder

Thunder is the loud noise that you hear in a storm. **Thunder** follows lightning.

tie

1. You **tie** something when you fasten the ends together.
2. A **tie** is something men wear around their shirt collars.

Aa Bb Cc Dd Ee Ff Gg Hh Ii Jj Kk Ll Mm

tiger

A **tiger** is a wild animal with black and orange stripes. **Tigers** are big cats.

tight

1. If clothes are too **tight**, they are not big enough.
2. If you hold something **tight**, you won't drop it.

time

We measure **time** in seconds, minutes, hours, days, weeks, months, and years. Look at the clock and see the **time**.

tiny

Things that are **tiny** are very, very small. Ants are **tiny** insects.

tired

If you feel **tired**, you want to rest or fall asleep.

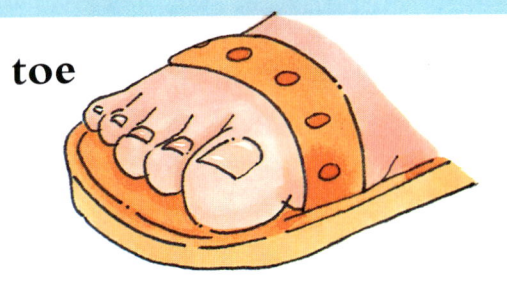

toe

Your **toes** are part of your body. You have five **toes** at the end of each foot.

tongue

Your **tongue** is inside your mouth. Your **tongue** helps you to speak and to taste food.

top

1. A **top** is a toy that turns very fast.
2. The **top** of something is its highest part.

tornado

A **tornado** is a very strong wind that turns fast in the air.

touch

When you **touch**, you feel things with your hands. Ice is cold to **touch**.

town

A **town** is a place where people live and work. **Towns** are smaller than cities.

toy

A **toy** is something you play with. A doll and a ball are both **toys**.

traffic

Traffic is automobiles and trucks traveling on the road. When there is a lot of **traffic**, the road is very busy.

train

Trains carry people and things quickly from one place to another. A **train** is pulled along by an engine.

tree

A **tree** is a very big plant with leaves and a trunk.

Nn Oo Pp Qq Rr Ss Tt Uu Vv Ww Xx Yy Zz

triangle

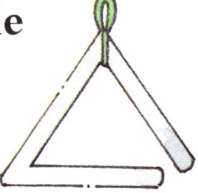

1. A **triangle** is a shape with three straight sides.
2. A **triangle** is something you can play music on.

truck

A **truck** is like a big strong car that carries things. **Trucks** travel on the road.

true

When something is **true**, it is right. **True** stories are about things that really happen.

try

If you **try** to do something, you see if you can do it. Joan will **try** to lift the heavy chair.

turn

1. When you **turn**, you move around in a circle.
2. When it is your **turn**, it is time for you to do something. It was Robert's **turn** to play.

Uu

uncle

Your father's brother and your mother's brother are your **uncles**.

understand

You **understand** when you know what something means. A dictionary helps you **understand** new words.

use

When you **use** a thing, you do something with it. Tammy **uses** a spoon to stir the soup.

Vv

valley

A **valley** is the low land between hills.

vegetable

A **vegetable** is a plant that you can eat. Carrots and potatoes are **vegetables** that grow under the ground.

video

A **video** has sound and pictures on it. To watch a **video**, you put it in a machine linked up to a television.

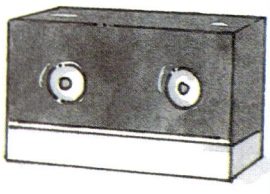

voice

Your **voice** is the sound you make when you speak or sing.

117

Aa Bb Cc Dd Ee Ff Gg Hh Ii Jj Kk Ll Mm

Ww

waist
Your **waist** is the middle part of your body, below your chest.

wait
When you **wait**, you stay where you are for a time. **Wait** here while I make a phone call.

walk
You **walk** by putting one foot in front of the other. Sometimes, Jamie **walks** to school.

wall 
1. The **walls** of a room are the sides of it.
2. Some gardens have **walls** around them.

want
When somebody **wants** something, they hope to get it. Melissa **wants** a new doll for her birthday.

warm
Warm is between hot and cold. Adam washed his face with **warm** water.

wash
When you **wash** something you use soap and water to clean it. Mandy helped Mom to **wash** the automobile.

watch
1. If you **watch** a person or a thing, you look to see what is happening. 
2. A **watch** is a small time-piece worn on your wrist.

water
There is **water** in seas and rivers. Fish live in **water**.

wave
1. When you **wave** to someone, you move your hand in the air. 
2. **Waves** are parts of the sea that move up and down.

way
1. The **way** somebody does something is how they do it.
2. The **way** to a place is how you get there.

weak
If people or things are **weak**, they are not very strong.

wear
1. When you **wear** something, you have it on your body.
2. When something **wears** out, it gets too old to use.

weather
The **weather** is how it is outside. It sometimes snows when the **weather** is cold.

week
A **week** is a measure of time. Seven days make one **week**.

118

Nn Oo Pp Qq Rr Ss Tt Uu Vv **Ww** Xx Yy Zz

weigh

You **weigh** something to find out how heavy it is. Dad **weighed** the sugar and flour when he made a cake.

wet

Something **wet** has water on it or in it.

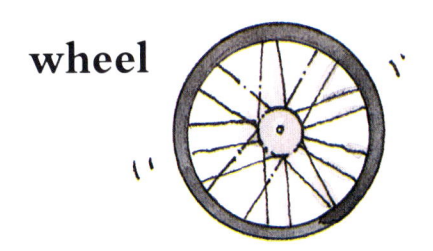

wheel

A **wheel** is round. Cars and bicycles move on **wheels**.

whisper

When you **whisper**, you say something very quietly.

whole

Whole means every part of something. Karen ate the **whole** cake.

wife

A **wife** is a woman who is married.

wild

If something is **wild**, it is not tame or quiet. Most **wild** animals live far from towns and cities.

win

When you **win**, you do best of all. Andrew **won** the swimming race.

wind

Wind is moving air. The strong **wind** blew the leaves from the trees.

window

A **window** is a space in a wall that lets in air and light. **Windows** have glass in them to keep out wind and rain.

wing

Birds and some insects have **wings**. They use their **wings** for flying.

wish

When you **wish** for something, you want it to happen.

wood

Wood comes from trees. It is used to make furniture, like tables and chairs.

wool

Wool is the coat of a sheep. People make **wool** into clothes.

word

People use **words** when they speak or write. "Cat," "funny," and "jump" are all **words**.

work

1. **Work** is a job that a person does for money. Dad **works** in a garage.
2. If something **works**, it is not broken. Mom mended the TV and now it **works**.

world

The **world** is the Earth that we all live on.

119

Nn Oo Pp Qq Rr Ss Tt Uu Vv **Ww Xx Yy Zz**

worry
When you **worry,** you think things will go wrong. Kate **worries** that she will be late for school.

write
When you **write,** you use a pen or pencil to make words on paper.

wrong
If something is **wrong,** it is not right. The answer to the question was **wrong**.

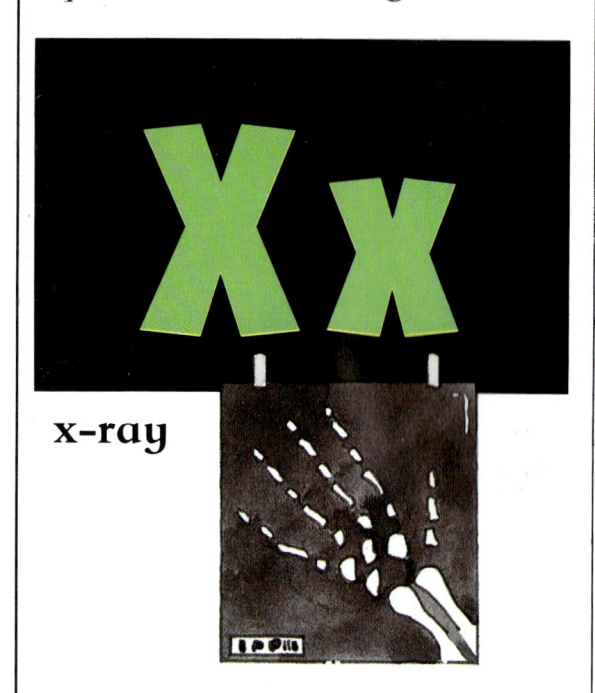

x-ray
An **x-ray** is a picture of the inside of a person's body.

yacht
A **yacht** is a kind of sailing boat. People race **yachts,** or sail in them for fun.

yard
A **yard** is a plot of land next to a house. Simon played in the **yard**.

year
A **year** is a measure of time. There are twelve months in a **year**. Neil will be seven **years** old next week.

young
If someone is **young,** they were born a short time ago. A kitten is a very **young** cat.

zebra
A **zebra** is a wild animal. **Zebras** look like horses with black and white stripes on their bodies.

zigzag
A **zigzag** is a line that bends one way and then the other.

zoo
A **zoo** is a place where wild animals are kept. People can see the animals in a **zoo**.